11/01

MULTIPLE INTELLIGENCES
and POSITIVE LIFE HABITS

MULTIPLE INTELLIGENCES
and POSITIVE LIFE HABITS

174 Activities for
Applying Them in Your Classroom

Lynne Beachner ■ Anola Pickett

CORWIN PRESS, INC.
A Sage Publications Company
2455 Teller Road
Thousand Oaks, CA 91320-2218
E-mail: order@corwinpress.com
Call: 800-818-7243 Fax: 800-4-1-SCHOOL
www.corwinpress.com

For information:

Corwin Press, Inc.
A Sage Publications Company
2455 Teller Road
Thousand Oaks, California 91320
E-mail: order@corwinpress.com

Sage Publications Ltd.
6 Bonhill Street
London EC2A 4PU
United Kingdom

Sage Publications India Pvt. Ltd.
M-32 Market
Greater Kailash I
New Delhi 110 048 India

Printed in the United States of America

Library of Congress Cataloging-in-Publication Data

Beachner, Lynne.
     Multiple intelligences and positive life habits: 174 activities for
applying them in your classroom / by Lynne Beachner and Anola Pickett.
          p.   cm.
     ISBN 0-7619-7727-9 (cloth) — ISBN 0-7619-7728-7 (pbk.)
     1. Education, Elementary—Activity programs.   2. Multiple intelligences.
   3. Cognitive styles in children.   I. Pickett, Anola.   II. Title.
     LB1592 .B43   2001
     372.13—dc21   00-012372

This book is printed on acid-free paper.

01   02   03   04   05   06   07   7   6   5   4   3   2   1

Acquiring Editor:	Faye Zucker
Corwin Editorial Assistant:	Julia Parnell
Production Editor:	Diane S. Foster
Editorial Assistant:	Cindy Bear
Typesetter/Designer:	Lynn Miyata
Indexer:	Molly Hall
Cover Designer:	Jane M. Quaney

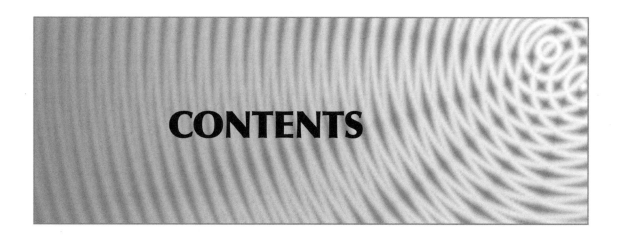

CONTENTS

Intrapersonal Intelligence / **102**

Reviewers

Anita Perry
Elementary Teacher
Leominster School District
Leominster, MA

Starr Hill
Parent Advocate/Educator
Franklin, VT

Diane Overton
Special Education Teacher
Las Virgenes Unified School District
Calabasas, CA

Dennis Wiseman
Dean, School of Education and Graduate Studies
Coastal Carolina University
Conway, SC

Jim Powell
National Director of Assessment and Evaluation
Kaplan Companies
Lewisville, NC

About the Authors

LYNNE BEACHNER, PhD, is principal of St. Francis Xavier School (SFX), in Kansas City, MO, and Adjunct Professor in the Department of Education, Rockhurst University (RU). In 1998, St. Francis Xavier School and Rockhurst University entered into a formal partnership to strengthen the curricular offerings at SFX and enhance the training of preservice teachers at Rockhurst. SFX is located across the street from RU so the sharing of resources and staff has been an exciting venture.

Prior to coming to St. Francis Xavier, Dr. Beachner was director and coauthor of a 3-year Federal Innovations in Education Grant implemented at Kansas Middle School of the Arts and Paseo Academy in the Kansas City, MO, School District. She also worked for the Kansas City School District as Coordinator of Instruction, was principal of Our Lady of the Presentation School, and taught students at the middle school level.

She lives with her husband, Gary Neal Johnson, a professional actor, and her two sons—Drew (10) and Ben (6)—who are a continued source of joy. The family enjoys reading, playing cards, attempting brain teasers, going to the theater, and camping.

ANOLA PICKETT is an educator and author. She holds a BA in English from Webster University and an MEd in Inner City Studies from Northeastern Illinois University. After teaching for more than 20 years in the preschool through college levels, she is currently the librarian at St. Francis Xavier School in Kansas City, MO. Her publication credits include *Old Enough for Magic,* a HarperCollins "I Can Read" book, and more than 50 stories, articles, and poems in magazines and newspapers. She lives with her husband, Peter Doyle, in Kansas City. Their son, Gerry Doyle, is a journalist.

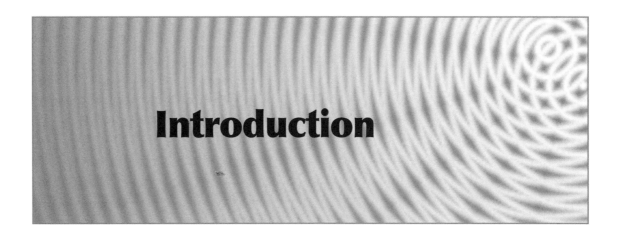

Introduction

Through many years of teaching and observing children and classrooms, we've found that the most successful teachers have two important qualities. First, they make an effort to know each child well, and second, they create a caring community within the classroom. With knowledge obtained from observing children, such teachers recognize each child's innate talents and work to enhance those strengths. As a result, their students feel successful and are more willing to take risks.

Very few talents are recognized and celebrated in schools. David is typical of those students whose ability is honored. David was savvy at discerning group relationships and feelings; he became the youngest student council president in the history of his school. Chris, a seventh grader, was so comfortable speaking in front of adults, he won membership on the school leadership team and traveled to another state to represent his school. Ashley, by nature very quiet, was the student others sought out when they wanted an unbiased opinion. And for those who felt down, Cassie could always offer solace. David and Chris's talents were recognized by the school because of their verbal and linguistic abilities. Ashley's intrapersonal skills and integrity were never acknowledged by the school; likewise, Cassie's caring nature and interpersonal talents received little recognition.

Schools reward what they value. The most common honors given at an annual elementary award assembly recognize perfect attendance, reading, spelling, and math skills. We are not proponents of awards assemblies. Instead, we would like to see children recognized daily for their creativity, their ability to solve problems, their knack for asking the right questions, their competency in designing and executing learning projects, their ability to find humor in a situation, their capacity for actively working for peace within a school community, and their passion for investigating many learning interests.

We wrote this book not to propose that more children receive public recognition, not to teach lessons in moral development—but to give teachers a toolbox enabling them to get to know their students in-depth and personally. With this knowledge, classrooms can celebrate the gifts of every student.

The Multiple Intelligence Approach

Howard Gardner, a professor at Harvard University and founder of Project Zero, has questioned the accepted use of IQ testing. Schools too often use IQ scores to determine the educational shortcomings of students, and in many cases these scores are used to advise students about their career choices. Traditional IQ tests measure language and mathematical abilities, but Gardner designed empirical studies to identify other ways people are intelligent. Schools, although traditionally resistant to change, have come to recognize the "rightness" of Gardner's theory, and many implement it in various ways. Proponents no longer ask, "Is this child intelligent?" but rather, "How is this child intelligent?" Although everyone has all the intelligences in varying degrees, Gardner's theory challenges us to find out how each child is gifted.

Gardner has identified eight intelligences:

- ◆ Verbal/Linguistic
- ◆ Mathematical/Logical
- ◆ Visual/Spatial
- ◆ Musical/Rhythmic
- ◆ Bodily/Kinesthetic
- ◆ Naturalist
- ◆ Interpersonal
- ◆ Intrapersonal

By using strategies that foster these intelligences, teachers can observe children working with concepts in meaningful ways—ways that provide more "aha" moments. When a highly musical child creates a song about an historical event or taps out the rhythm of vocabulary words, he or she is more likely to succeed.

A Case for Teaching Life Habits

Recently, people have grown concerned about the decline of positive life habits among youth. In his book *Emotional Intelligence* (1995), Daniel Goleman points out that emotional intelligence may predict about 80% accurately whether a person will be successful in life. Rachel Kessler wrote *The Soul of Education: Helping Students Find Connection, Compassion and Character at School* (2000); Susan Kovalik stresses the importance of "lifeskills" in *ITI the Model* (1994); the Association for Supervision and Curriculum Development (ASCD) devoted an issue of *Educational Leadership* (May, 1997) to "Social and Emotional Learning." These authors stress the need for schools to recognize there is more to curriculum than facts. Children must learn to get along with each other and share some common beliefs about relationships.

It is also important for teachers to develop relationships with students and to aid them in developing a sense of connectedness with a group. Schools must expand the notion of "reading, 'riting, & 'rithmetic" to include "relationships." Life Habits need to be part of a proactive plan to teach students problem solving skills and positive interactions. These habits must become the common language in schools. Teachers need to point out when they see a Life Habit modeled. They need to discuss the Life Habits used in current events or in the literature they're studying with their students. Above all, teachers themselves must visibly model positive Life Habits in their own daily interactions with students and adults.

How to Use This Book

We hope you use these activities in this book as a guide to incorporate Life Habits and Gardner's intelligences into your curriculum as teaching/learning strategies. We have included many activities that can be used directly in content areas. Other activities deal specifically with developing classroom community. The book is organized into eight chapters, each focusing on one Multiple Intelligence. In addition, "Life Habits Breakdown" assists you in finding the Life Habit activities just right for your class and grade level. The Breakdown is divided according to specific Life Habit and includes a description of activities and their appropriate grade level. Choose activities suited to your classroom and vary the Multiple Intelligence approach.

Some activities are designed specifically for the beginning of the year. The activity "Visioning" can be used to help students set personal goals. To facilitate children in getting to know each other, use activities such as "Introductions," "Getting to Know You," "Friendly Form," "BUDDYO," and/or "Eye to Eye." To build group identity you might use "Class Song" and "Motto Making." To familiarize students with the Life Habits, try "Going Once, Going Twice, Sold!" or "It's Like . . ." or "Creature Stew." A copy of the Life Habits Overview can be inserted into a student handbook, journal notebook, procedure book, or any binder to which students have easy access. Student groups can make posters of the five major Life Habits areas to be hung in the room.

Each activity has discussion and journal questions. Do not skip this component. Activity without reflection loses its value. Make sure your group processes the activity and that everyone self-reflects through journaling. Make up your own questions as you get to know your students better, or ask students to make up journal questions. Make sure you read the activity "The Talking Stick." This technique can be used in conjunction with other activities as a management tool.

Relationships

From the moment we are born, we begin forming relationships with other human beings, and we continue to do so all our lives. Relationships both contribute to mental health and are affected by mental health. These five Life Habits begin with the relationship one has with oneself and extend to relationships with others.

Teamwork

Today's workplace is often built around a team approach, and the most effective way to create social or political change is to work with others. These Life Habits facilitate working to achieve a common goal through effective communication, treating everyone equitably, and working with all members of the team.

Common Sense

Success in everyday life requires common sense. Simple courtesy with friends, family, and coworkers; stopping for a red light; organizing ingredients for dinner—life is filled with thousands of commonsense actions and decisions. These four Life Habits all concern patterns that foster calm and order.

Productivity

To get any job done—a simple household chore, winning a game, or creating a higher profit margin—productivity is required. Those who have an internal desire to do well and finish feel more satisfied at the end of a project, and their work is usually more thorough and correct. These four Life Habits deal with a person's desire to finish the task and accomplish the goal.

Problem Solving

Life is filled with decisions; some are minor; some are life-changing. What to wear? How to save money? When to study? Usually there are several answers, often found by stepping outside the usual patterns of thinking. Problem-solving practice early in life enables us to see options and make more difficult choices as an adult. These Life Habits deal with thinking patterns and how we find and try solutions.

Overview of Life Habits

Relationships

• Self-Awareness	Knowledge of your own feelings, habits, and beliefs
Sense of Humor	Seeing and enjoying the funny side of life without making others feel uncomfortable or put down
Caring	Developing a positive connection with another person
Integrity	Remaining true to your own feelings, habits, and beliefs
Respect	Honoring the worth of another person

Teamwork

Communication	Delivering information and/or feelings in an effective way
Active Listening	Receiving information and/or feelings in a mindful, active manner
Cooperation	Actively working with the whole group to reach the goal
Patience	Focusing on the goal even when there are problems
Fair Play	Treating others as you want to be treated

Common Sense

Alertness	Staying aware of what's going on around you
Accountability	Performing your part in an activity
Organization	Arranging things in a workable order
Courtesy	Expressing manners through words or actions

Productivity

Initiative	Acting from your own desire to reach a goal
Perseverance/Effort	Continuing to work until the goal is reached
Responsibility	Doing your job well and completely
Motivation	Finding a positive reason for reaching the goal and encouraging others
Courage	Working at the task, even when there are problems

Problem Solving

Creativity	Looking at a problem and its solutions in a new way
Flexibility/Resilience	Trying another way if something doesn't work
Curiosity	Desiring to know more about things
Confidence	Believing you can do what you need to do

Life Habits Breakdown

Relationships

Title	*Grade*	*Description*	*MI*
		SELF-AWARENESS	
Visioning	K & Up	Students reflect on what they would like to be	Intra
10 Things	K & Up	10 things students would like to do with life	Intra
Personal Statement	K & Up	Students design T-shirts	Intra
Business Card	K & Up	Students market their good qualities	Intra
My Circle of Circles	2 & Up	Students list their connections to groups	M/L
Put Your Name Up	3 & Up	Class makes name posters	Inter
What's Bugging You?	K & Up	Students list things that bug them	M/L
Space Zone 1	K & Up	Exercise on personal space	Intra
Space Zone 2	K & Up	Students mark their personal spaces with yarn	Intra
		SENSE OF HUMOR	
Japanese Portrait Game	1 & Up	Students do blind drawings of their faces	V/S
Skediddle Daddle	3 & Up	Class learns names	Inter
Four Up	2 & Up	Only four people standing at a time	B/K
Train Station	4 & Up	Students wave to the wrong people	B/K
The Balloon Popper	2 & Up	Students sit on each other's balloons	B/K
Punctuate the Point	4 & Up	Groups come up with movement, gesture, & sound for punctuation	B/K
Elbow Shake	1 & Up	Students shake hands in different positions	B/K
Presto-Chango!	3 & Up	Students study each other, then change four things	V/S

Title	Grade	Description	MI
CARING			
Play It Again, Sam!	3 & Up	Students give two compliments for one put-down	Inter
STARS	4 & Up	Students make one positive statement about each classmate	Inter
Look on the Sunny Side	4 & Up	Class puts positive statements on paper plates	V/S
"I Spy" a Good Deed	2 & Up	Students catch classmates being good	Inter
Getting to Know You	3 & Up	Students interview classmates	Inter
Caring Cards	3 & Up	Students write sentences to show friendship	V/L
INTEGRITY			
Favorites	3 & Up	Students find others who have same "favorites"	Intra
"DOTS"	3 & Up	Students silently find their "dot" color group	B/K
Peer Pressure	2 & Up	Students convince others with opposing instructions	Inter
Stop, Look, and Listen	4 & Up	Teams describe "integrity"	V/S
What Will Happen?	3 & Up	Students come up with an individual & a group solution	Intra
Yes, No, Maybe So, Certainly	2 & Up	Students practice making decisions	Intra
Choose Your Card	K & Up	Students finish the sentence, "I would rather . . . "	Intra
I Used to . . . but Now I . . .	K & Up	Students say how they've changed	Intra
Go-Around	K & Up	Students answer questions—one at a time	Intra
What Should We Buy?	3 & Up	Pairs decide on three items they want to buy	M/L
Guess What!	2 & Up	Prearrange trick—two students leave room	V/L

Life Habits Breakdown *(continued)*

Title	Grade	Description	MI
RESPECT			
Polite Hang-ups	2 & Up	Mobile of courtesy & respect	V/S
Toe to Toe *26*	2 & Up	Students change roles	V/L
How Do You See This?	2 & Up	Students list important things from a picture	Intra
If I Weren't Here	1 & Up	If not here, where? Students match others	Intra
Empathy Exercise	4 & Up	Students finish the sentence & solve problem, "A problem I'm working on is . . ."	Intra
Culture Clash	4 & Up	Four cultures interact	Inter
Wall of Fame	K & Up	Class identifies each student's talents	Intra

Common Sense

Title	Grade	Description	Page
ALERTNESS			
Classroom Conducting	2 & Up	Students conduct music	M/R
Birthday Search	3 & Up	Students try to find others with the same birthday	B/K
One . . . Two . . . Clap!	1 & Up	Class sings a song—clapping on third beat	M/R
Pass the Number, Please	5 & Up	Students add numbers to sequence	M/L
Never Say "I"	3 & Up	Students speak on a topic without saying, "I, me, my, or mine"	V/L
Mirror Pairs	3 & Up	Students match movements	B/K
High Card Wins!	1 & Up	Students treat each other according to status	M/L
Detective!	3 & Up	Class detectives solve a mystery	V/L
Sounds of Silence	3 & Up	Students list sounds they hear around them	M/R
Strike Up the Band!	1 & Up	Class divides into orchestra and dancers	M/R
Sword Game	3 & Up	Everyone reacts to sword fight	B/K
Mood Music	3 & Up	Students listen to music and identify mood	M/R

Title	Grade	Description	MI
ALERTNESS (continued)			
Animal Search	3 & Up	Students find others with the same animal—act it out while others guess	N
Rubbings	K & Up	Class explores textures of things in nature	N
The Memory Game	2 & Up	Students memorize objects on a table	M/L
ACCOUNTABILITY			
Infinite Circle	6 & Up	Students stay on boards in a circle	B/K
Photo Finish	4 & Up	Team members cross finish line at exactly the same time	B/K
Tree Scavenger Hunt	5 & Up	Class identifies local trees	N
Environmental Orchestra	1 & Up	Groups choose sounds from environment to play and conduct	M/R
ORGANIZATION			
Nature at the Gallery	2 & Up	Class looks for nature in works of art	N
Balloon Castle	6 & Up	Class builds a structure	M/L
The House	4 & Up	Class builds house shape with rope	M/L
The Star	4 & Up	Class creates a 5-point star with rope	V/S
Team Name Puzzle	3 & Up	Students connect their first names in acrostic puzzle	V/L
Four of a Kind	3 & Up	Students discover similarities & differences	V/L
All Aboard!!!	2 & Up	Students build consensus	Inter
Building a Shelter	5 & Up	Class uses tape & newspaper to build a shelter	V/S
Bring the Outdoors In	2 & Up	Class decides how the outdoors can be in the classroom	N
Recipe for a Perfect Environment	4 & Up	Students develop ways to maintain a perfect environment	N
Creative Measurement	3 & Up	Students create and use their own unit of measurement	M/L
Picture This	K & Up	Students tell a story through series of pictures	N

Life Habits Breakdown *(continued)*

Title	Grade	Description	MI
COURTESY			
Simple Solutions	4 & Up	Students open their partners' fists	Inter
Introductions	3 & Up	Students introduce each other	Inter
Roundabout Conversations	1 & Up	Students form a circle & do introductions when the music stops	Inter
Reaching Out	2 & Up	Class reaches out to someone who . . .	B/K

Productivity

Title	Grade	Description	Page
INITIATIVE			
Bear-Hunter-Cage	4 & Up	Team decisions (like Scissors-Paper-Rock)	B/K
Pretzel Puzzle	K & Up	Circle of students ties self into knot	M/L
Take Me to Your Leader	3 & Up	Class sings a song in a circle—with no leader	M/R
It's Like . . .	3 & Up	Students choose & interpret a Life Habit	V/S
PERSEVERANCE			
Friendly Web	1 & Up	Students create a maze with yarn around a person, then undo it	V/S
Laugh-In	2 & Up	Team tries to "crack up" opposite team	Inter
Myth Nature	3 & Up	Students create a myth to explain natural phenomena	N
"All Together Now . . ."	K & Up	All stand using a rope	B/K
The Plus and the Zero	K & Up	Students draw a plus sign & a zero at the same time	B/K
Pendulum Pairs	2 & Up	Pairs keep the beat of a pendulum	M/R
CAN DO!	K & Up	Students practice saying, "I CAN"	Intra

Title	Grade	Description	MI
RESPONSIBILITY			
The Four Elements	4 & Up	Students characterize air, earth, fire, or water	N
If I Had an Angel	2 & Up	Each student is assigned to be another's angel	Intra
Animal Art	K & Up	Students create a collage with objects from nature	N
Saving for a Rainy Day	5 & Up	Students choose the best way to save money	M/L
Litter Patrol	2 & Up	Class picks up litter on the school grounds	N
COURAGE			
Speedy Solutions	5 & Up	Students come up with quick solutions to problems	Inter
Open Mike	4 & Up	Class watches 5 circle up and discuss problem	V/L
The Power Chair	3 & Up	Chairs arranged to show who has power	V/S
Please Tell Me That I . . .	1 & Up	Students say what they'd like to hear about themselves	Intra
MOTIVATION			
YES! YES! YES!	K & Up	Circle of students stand saying, "Yes"	B/K
Chain of Links	2 & Up	Students form a chain of goals reached	V/S
Racing Chain	2 & Up	Teams follow stepping "stones" one at a time	B/K
I Think I Can	3 & Up	Students give suggestions to help others reach goals	Intra
Let's Have a Party!	3 & Up	Class follows directions to prepare for a party	M/L
Protector Shield	3 & Up	Students choose a protector against a foe	B/K
The Teaching Song	3 & Up	Students use a song to learn rules	M

Life Habits Breakdown (continued)

Teamwork

Title	Grade	Description	MI
COMMUNICATION			
The Talking Stick	K & Up	Class passes it around for discussions	V/L
BUDDYO	4 & Up	Students gather names & play Bingo	Inter
Claymotion	K & Up	Class sculpts emotions	V/S
Give Me an "A"!	3 & Up	Group spells a word with their bodies	B/K
What Was That Again?	3 & Up	Class watches a silent comedy	B/K
Taxicab!!!!	3 & Up	Groups of three, two form a seat for the third with their arms	B/K
ACTIVE LISTENING			
Name Toss	1 & Up	Students pass a ball—repeat pattern—say their names	Inter
Compliment Relay	3 & Up	Students say a complimentary addition about the person behind them	V/L
Friendly Form	3 & Up	Students find others who share the same things	Inter
Gossip	4 & Up	Students whisper a story & pass it around	V/L
Who's the Star?	K & Up	Students find the right person by how loudly others clap	M/R
I Like Anyone Who . . .	K & Up	Musical chairs with words	B/K
Triple Listening	2 & Up	Students summarize others, then speak	V/L
Round Robin	1 & Up	Class finishes statements	Intra
Walking Warm-ups	1 & Up	Students walk according to directions	B/K
Categories	1 & Up	Students read lists then categorize items	V/L

Title	*Grade*	*Description*	*MI*
ACTIVE LISTENING (continued)			
You Say, I Say	K & Up	Students make and repeat statements	V/L
Musical Grab Bag	1 & Up	Students repeat music with instruments	M/R
COOPERATION			
Partner Drawing	5 & Up	Students take turns drawing a picture—one stroke at a time	V/S
Collaborative Poem	3 & Up	Each student writes one line—shuffle—make a poem	V/L
The Machine	1 & Up	Students build a machine by adding one movement to another	B/K
Silhouette	K & Up	Students' bodies form an event, story, etc.	B/K
Symbol Silhouette	5 & Up	Group puts things they think, see, hear, etc., on a student's body outline	V/S
Geometeam	5 & Up	Team makes polygons with rope	M/L
Skyscraper	2 & Up	Students build a tall structure	M/L
Class Song	4 & Up	Students develop a class song	M/R
Musical Chair Cooperation	K & Up	Students can sit on each other's laps	M/R
Eat Up!	1 & Up	Students attach sticks to their writing arms	Inter
How Many Can You Think Of?	3 & Up	Class brainstorms items for a category	V/L
The Birthday Line	3 & Up	Class makes a timeline of their birthdays—without talking	B/K
PATIENCE			
Coop Squares	5 & Up	Students count the total number of squares	M/L
Group Knot	3 & Up	Class grabs hands then untangles knot	B/K
Building With Cards	2 & Up	Students build a three-story structure with cards	V/S
Place Percussion	K & Up	Class claps the rhythms of words	M/R

Life Habits Breakdown (continued)

Title	Grade	Description	MI
FAIR PLAY			
Arm Wrestling	3 & Up	Students try to get touchdowns	Inter
The Trust Circle	3 & Up	Class makes a circle—some lean in & some lean out	B/K
Pandora's Box	4 & Up	Students resolve conflicts	Inter
Cats 'n Dogs	K & Up	Students design a way to keep cats and dogs from fighting	V/S

Problem Solving

Title	Grade	Description	Page
CREATIVITY			
Bouts Rimes	K & Up	Students write poems using rhyming words	V/L
Invent A Game	3 & Up	Students create a game with given objects	Inter
Truth Detector	3 & Up	Students talk about themselves & tell one lie—others guess	Inter
What Do You Think?	3 & Up	Students brainstorm uses of selected item	Inter
Build a Better Bike	K & Up	Students brainstorm with DOVE rule	V/S
Creature Stew	4 & Up	Students pick a Life Habit and give it physical attributes	V/S
Motto Making	3 & Up	Students design a flag and motto for the group	V/S
Space Invention	2 & Up	Students create an environment with set objects	V/S
This Is the Way We . . .	2 & Up	Students create a sentence song	M/R
Season Scenes	2 & Up	Groups create a tableau of a season	N

Title	Grade	Description	MI
CREATIVITY (continued)			
Flying High	K & Up	Students pretend they are flying & describe it	N
Weather Forecast	3 & Up	Students make up a riddle about a weather word	N
Creature Match	K & Up	Students identify creatures for each "intelligence"	N
FLEXIBILITY/RESILIENCE			
Crescendo	4 & Up	Students mirror sound and motion & build it	M/R
Wrap-a-Long	2 & Up	Wrap teams in plastic then race	B/K
The Puzzler	5 & Up	Groups discover missing puzzle pieces in other groups	Inter
Building in a Box	3 & Up	Groups plan buildings then open box of materials they must use	Inter
Clap Along	K & Up	Class claps until a pattern emerges	M/R
CURIOSITY			
Danger!!	4 & Up	Students face danger by bringing person from history to their aid	N
What's in a Name?	4 & Up	Students combine their names & make words	V/L
Who's the Leader?	4 & Up	"It" leaves then returns & guesses leader of sounds & moves	B/K
Rock Game	3 & Up	Students bond with and introduce rock	N
What in the World?	1 & Up	Students interpret paint blots	V/S
Art Quest	4 & Up	Class makes observations from paintings	V/S
Eye to Eye	K & Up	Students find five things in common and five different	V/S
Class-O-Graph	3 & Up	Students decide what to ask classmates	M/L
Nature Quest	K & Up	Class brainstorms questions about nature & research	N

Life Habits Breakdown *(continued)*

Title	Grade	Description	MI
CONFIDENCE			
Bean Jar	4 & Up	Students guess the number of beans—as individuals, then in dyads, quartets, etc.	M/L
Pig Latin Review	3 & Up	Students ask questions & interpret Pig Latin	V/L
Touch & Spin	3 & Up	Partners spin then reestablish contact with partner	B/K
Vote With Your Feet	K & Up	Students choose an area and move to it	Intra
Going Once, Going Twice, Sold!	4 & Up	Groups buy Life Habits at auction	M/L

1 Verbal/Linguistic Intelligence

Children strong in this intelligence have highly developed auditory skills and enjoy language activities. They tend to think in words rather than pictures and can usually be found reading a book or writing a story or poem. They make good storytellers and are often good speakers and actors. These children learn best through verbalizing, seeing, or hearing words. This intelligence is the one most widely shared by all human beings.

Look for children who like to write; tell tall tales, jokes, and stories; easily remember names, places, dates, or trivia; enjoy reading books for pleasure; are good spellers; appreciate nonsense rhymes and tongue twisters; like crossword puzzles or games such as Scrabble and Up-Words.

To nurture Verbal/Linguistic Intelligence, encourage the reading and writing of poems, advertisements, biographies, books, news stories, brochures, instructions, crossword puzzles, journals, editorials, essays, metaphors, fact files, greeting cards, fairy tales, letters, literary magazines, reports, quizzes or worksheets, speeches, plays, and skits.

What's in a Name?

Multiple Intelligence: Verbal/Linguistic   **Grade: 4 and Up**
Life Habit: Curiosity   **Time: 10 minutes, including directions**
Materials: Paper and pencils

1. Class should be in groups of 4 or 5 students each. Ask the students in each group to write all of their names on a piece of paper.

2. Each group then tries to make as many words as possible from the combined letters in the names. Words should be three or more letters long. No proper names or foreign words are allowed. (Rules may be changed to suit the group.)

3. Give the students 3 minutes to find words. If desired, change the composition of the groups and try another round.

Example   These names (Sarah, Bill, Linda, Andrew) contain these words (sail, ill, blind, dare, drew, land, and wad).

Discussion 1. How did your group begin looking for words?

2. Did people just jump in with suggestions, or did you take turns? What worked best? Did everyone participate?

Journal   How does curiosity help us see something in a different way? Give an example.

Bouts Rimes

Multiple Intelligence: Verbal/Linguistic   **Grade: K and Up**
Life Habit: Creativity   **Time: 30 minutes**
Materials: Writing materials

1. This was a popular game in the courts of the French kings 350 years ago. Divide students into groups of 3 to 5 students each. Each group makes up two pairs of common rhyming words.

2. Their job is then to write a poem using their words.

Example   If the rhyming pairs are **lake/cake** and **rare/care**, this poem could result:

> *We ate our cake*
> *By the deep blue lake.*
> *The cake was rare*
> *And we learned to care.*

Variation   Teams pass their rhyming words to other groups to see how many different poems can result.

Discussion 1. Why do you think this game was popular?

2. Was it hard to find ways to connect the rhyming words?

Journal   1. Write down your favorite Bouts Rimes from class today. Explain why they were your favorites.

2. Write another poem using the words **day/pay** and **dog/fog**.

How Many Things Can You Think Of?

Multiple Intelligence: Verbal/Linguistic　　　　**Grade: 3 and Up**
Life Habit: Cooperation　　　　　　　　　　　**Time: 10 to 15 minutes**
Materials: Paper and pencils

1. Arrange students into groups of 4. One student should be the group scribe.

2. Give students a category, such as "things bigger than you are," "things taller than a car," "things with handles," "things made from wood," and so on. Ask them to think of as many things as they can to fit that description.

3. The group scribe should write the ideas as they are given. The group can make their own rules about the best way and order to present ideas. Assign a 3- to 5-minute time limit .

4. Allow each group to share their list with the rest of the class.

1. Did your group give ideas faster than the scribe could write them down? How did you solve that problem?

Discussion

2. Did your group have an idea different from any of the other groups?

3. Did you hear some ideas you wish you had thought of?

Does this kind of activity work better in a group rather than alone? Explain.

Journal

Triple Listening

Multiple Intelligence: Verbal/Linguistic　　　　**Grade: 2 and Up**
Life Habit: Active Listening　　　　　　　　　**Time: 15 to 20 minutes**
Materials: None

1. Arrange the students into groups of 3. Explain that in this activity all students have a chance to speak, but before they do so, they must repeat or sum up what the person who just spoke said. The previous speaker must agree the summary is correct. Allow about 3 minutes per speaker.

2. Ask each group to select Person 1, who will be the first to speak; Person 2, who will be the listener; and Person 3, who will be the observer. Give the students a simple topic to speak about, one about which children of the age you teach have an opinion. (e.g., Should

our school have a dress code? Should we be allowed to eat in the classroom? Should we be allowed to chew gum in school?)

3. After Person 1 has spoken, Person 2 summarizes.

4. When Person 3 and Person 1 agree that the summary is correct, then it is Person 2's turn to speak. Person 1 becomes the observer, and Person 3 becomes the listener.

5. Repeat this process until all three students in each group have had the chance to speak.

Discussion

1. What was the most difficult job—speaker, listener, or observer—in the group? Why?

2. If a speaker disagreed with the summary, what did the group do?

Journal   Describe a situation in real life in which listening accurately could be very important. What could happen if the listener did not hear the information correctly?

Categories

Multiple Intelligence: Verbal/Linguistic   **Grade: 1 and Up**
Life Habit: Active Listening   **Time: 10 to 15 minutes**
Materials: Paper and pencils

1. Ask students to work in pairs. Depending upon their age, ask students to make 2 to 5 columns on their paper. Give them a category for each column. Then read a list of words and ask them to agree on the column to which the word belongs.

2. They should write the words in the columns they have agreed upon. For a quicker, simpler version, ask them to mark an X in the correct column. This exercise can be as simple or as complicated as you care to make it. It can also be used to review vocabulary words.

Discussion

1. Was it difficult to quickly decide where a word belonged?

2. Could some words belong in more than one category? Give examples.

Journal   Are there times in life when you have to make a quick decision about something? Describe one of these times that you have experienced.

You Say, I Say

Multiple Intelligence: Verbal/Linguistic   **Grade: K and Up**
Life Habit: Active Listening   **Time: 15 to 20 minutes**
Materials: None

1. Ask the students to sit or stand in a circle. Ask for a volunteer to begin, or choose one. The first student makes a personal statement, such as "My favorite food is_____."

2. The student to the right of the speaker repeats what the first person has said and then makes his or her own statement about the topic. This continues around the circle, with each student repeating what the previous student has said before making his or her own statement.

1. What was the most difficult part of this activity?   **Discussion**

2. Did you learn anything that surprised you?

Is it more difficult for you to talk about yourself or listen to others?   **Journal**
Why do you think this is true? Do you think it's true of most people?
Why?

Collaborative Poem

Multiple Intelligence: Verbal/Linguistic   **Grade: 3 and Up**
Life Habit: Cooperation   **Time: 30 minutes**
Materials: Strips of paper, pens, one long sheet
   of paper (or section of bulletin board)

1. Give a strip of paper and a pen to each participant. Direct each person to write one phrase or sentence on the paper. The writing should include a color, an animal, and a place (or any three items of your choice). When all poets are finished, collect the strips.

2. Ask a student to shuffle the strips.

3. Call students up, one at a time, and give them a strip. Ask them to tape their strips to the long piece of paper, one after the other.

4. When all the strips are in place, read the poem aloud.

1. What would be a good title for the poem?   **Discussion**

2. Are you pleased with the outcome? Should some strips be moved?

Choose any five lines from those the class wrote. Put them together to   **Journal**
make your own personal poem, adding some of your own lines.

Gossip

Multiple Intelligence: Verbal/Linguistic
Life Habit: Active Listening
Materials: None
Time: 5 to 10 minutes, depending upon size of group

Grade: 4 and Up
(and younger students
with a simpler story)

1. Seat students in a circle. Explain that a story will be whispered to one member of the circle and then passed on around the circle. The last person to hear the story then repeats it aloud to the whole group.

2. Whisper the story to the student next to you in the circle. After it has gone around the circle, discuss how accurately the story was passed.

Story 1   Marvinnetta Morris, who is 88 years old, lives in Mason, Missouri, with her macaw Mo. She enjoys skating in her bathtub but has trouble keeping the water frozen.

Story 2   In the year 2055, maroon Martians landed on earth. They were ugly, with green faces, 14 arms, 4 heads, 5 ears, watermelon legs and prune feet. They landed in New York City and went to the zoo. Their first words were, "Who ordered pizza?"

Discussion   1. How did you feel when the story got to you? Did it make any sense?

2. What did you do to try to make sense out of it?

Journal   Write about a rumor passed along from one neighbor to another, ending up with its being told to the first person, who doesn't recognize it and starts another rumor.

Open Mike

Multiple Intelligence: Verbal/Linguistic
Life Habit: Courage
Materials: None

Grade: 4 and Up
Time: 40 minutes

1. Place six chairs in a circle in the middle or front of the room. Announce to students that you would like five volunteers to sit in the circle to discuss their views on a specific topic (you decide on and inform students about the topic before they volunteer). The extra chair is the "open mike" seat. It may be occupied by any member of the class who wants to add his or her "two cents" to the conversation. After giving an opinion, the person should return to his or her seat.

2. The topic needs to be discussed by the five members before it is opened to the larger group. The teacher should determine when others are to be invited into the circle.

1. Any current events topic.

2. Do peers influence your behavior? If so, to what extent? What are the limits of their influence?

3. If you were to design your own school, what would it be like?

4. Some people believe that if students wore uniforms, the climate of the school would improve. What are the pros and cons?

Possible Topics

1. Did you change your opinion on the topic as a result of listening to the conversation?

2. Did the option of joining the discussion encourage you to be more involved in the conversation?

3. Did it take courage to join the group?

Discussion

1. Being outside (inside) the circle, I felt . . .

2. I wanted to say . . .

Journal

Compliment Relay

Multiple Intelligence: Verbal/Linguistic　　　　**Grade: 3 and Up**
Life Habit: Active Listening　　　　　　　　　**Time: As needed**
Materials: None

1. Ask the class to line up in rows of five students each. The first student uses a complimentary adjective to describe the person behind him or her. The compliment should be something about the person, not about the person's clothing or hairstyle. An example is, "I think you are very creative."

2. The second person turns to the third person and repeats the first compliment and adds another compliment. For example, "I think you are very creative and kind."

3. The third person turns to the fourth and adds a compliment; the fourth turns to the fifth and adds a compliment; and the fifth student repeats aloud all the compliments that have been passed to him or her. The rest of the row checks to see if all the compliments have been correctly passed on.

Choose one student each day. Ask the rest of the class to compliment that student.

Variation

Discussion   How did you feel while listening to the compliments being passed along?

Journal   Sometimes people give each other phony or empty compliments. Is this ever a good idea? Can it cause problems? Explain.

The Talking Stick

Multiple Intelligence: Verbal/Linguistic   **Grade: K and Up**
Life Habit: Communication   **Time: As needed**
Materials: A talking stick made from a tree branch, 12 to 15 inches long, and about 1 inch thick; strip of leather; feather tied to stick with leather

1. The Talking Stick can be used on a regular basis to discuss a question, issue, or problem or to introduce new material.

2. The Talking Stick is passed around the group, beginning in the area of the room where the sun rises. Whoever holds the stick may speak to the issue; no one else may speak. A person always has the option to skip a turn and pass the stick without speaking.

3. Continue until the Talking Stick has completed the circle; make another circuit if members still wish to speak or if those who passed now wish to say something.

4. If desired, you may establish a time limit and a signal word to mark the end of a turn, such as "Teamwork!" or "Peace!"

Discussion   Because the Talking Stick is a discussion device used on an ongoing basis, no specific discussion topics are provided.

Journal   Imagine you are the Talking Stick. Write a story about what you've heard in a particular situation or discussion.

Never Say "I"

Multiple Intelligence: Verbal/Linguistic   **Grade: 3 and Up**
Life Habit: Alertness   **Time: 8 to 10 minutes**
Materials: None

1. Have players pair up and stand facing each other. Announce a topic for discussion and explain that one partner begins talking about the topic to the other partner, but may not use the words **I, My, Me,** or **Mine** as he or she talks.

2. Change speakers every 20 or 30 seconds.

3. If a player uses one of the forbidden words, the player must sit down, and his or her partner looks for another partner. This continues until only one person is left standing.

◆ The most important person in my life

◆ My summer vacation

◆ My favorite singing group

◆ Why I believe in democracy

Possible Topics

Why was it difficult to avoid using these words? Would different topics have made it easier? Why?

Discussion

Choose a letter of the alphabet. Or, to make it more difficult, ask someone else to choose a letter. Try to write a paragraph without using that letter. Was this difficult? Why? What letters would be easiest to leave out? Why?

Journal

Detective!

Multiple Intelligence: Verbal/Linguistic
Life Habit: Alertness
Materials: Blackboard

Grade: 3 and Up
Time: 15 to 20 minutes

1. Divide the class into two teams. Ask a volunteer from each team to be the detective.

2. The detectives stand so they cannot see the blackboard. They can also stand at the back of the room so they cannot receive visual clues from their teammates.

3. Write a situation on the board, such as, "The school must be on fire."

4. Next, ask the teams to take turns giving clues. The clues may not contain the main words of the sentence on the board. Using our example, clues might include:
   – "I can smell smoke."
   – "It's getting hotter in here."
   – "The alarm is ringing."
   – "People are jumping out of the windows."

5. After each clue, the detectives have a chance to guess the situation.

Discussion
1. Was it difficult to think of clues without giving away the answer? Why?

2. Do you think it was easier to be the detective or a clue-giver?

Journal
Describe a time when you used clues to figure out something or a time when you gave someone else clues to make her or him guess about something.

Toe to Toe

Multiple Intelligence: Verbal/Linguistic **Grade: 2 and Up**
Life Habit: Respect **Time: 10 to 15 minutes**
Materials: None

1. Have your students form two lines, facing each other. Each student should be opposite another student. Name one line A and the other line B.

2. Describe a problem situation involving two persons, A and B. Some examples are:
   ◆ Person A wants to go to a movie and Person B wants to go to the mall.
   ◆ Person A says, "I have a right to cut in line, " but Person B says, "No one should cut in front of me."
   ◆ Person A feels that girls are smarter than boys, and Person B feels that boys are smarter than girls.

3. Explain that when you say "Begin," the students should assume their roles as Person A or Person B and begin to gesture, talk, and use facial expressions to act out their roles.

4. Continue for 2 minutes. Tell the students then to reverse roles in the situation. Again, say "Begin!" and they should start up again, acting out their new roles for 2 minutes. You may continue with a new problem situation if you wish.

Discussion
1. How did you feel when you had to change roles and play the other part?

2. Was this difficult to do? Why or why not?

Journal
Is it important to be able to take the other side in a problem or argument? Why?

Guess What!

Multiple Intelligence: Verbal/Linguistic
Life Habit: Integrity
Materials: None

Grade: 2 and Up
Time: 15 minutes

1. Before class, choose one student to be your "accomplice." Tell your accomplice you will always name a four-legged animal just before the correct answer. For example, if the answer is "flower," you could give the following list of words—cabinet, radio, dog, flower. "Dog" comes before "flower," so "flower" is the answer.

2. Choose your accomplice and one other student to leave the room.

3. The class should agree on a "secret" word.

4. When the two students return to the room, tell them their job is to guess the "secret" word. Begin by saying a series of words, making sure to say the name of a four-legged animal just before the "secret" word. This can be repeated as many times as you like.

_____ (the accomplice) did an amazing job of guessing the answer. It really beats all the odds. How do you think he or she did that? You came up with the words. There was no way for him or her to hear the words and for _____ (the other student) not to hear the same words. Is this just a special talent? Let's do it again. This time, look for patterns. (Repeat the process and then discuss the patterns found.)

Discussion

Ask _____ (the other student), "How did you feel when _____ (the accomplice) got all the answers and you didn't? How did you feel when you found out it was a trick? If you had found out from someone else, would you have had the same feelings?"

1. Why is it important to be honest with others?

Journal

2. Have you ever not been totally honest and it was found out? What happened as a result? How did you feel?

Caring Cards

Multiple Intelligence: Verbal/Linguistic
Life Habit: Caring
Materials: One index card for each student, pens or pencils

Grade: 3 and Up
Time: 10 minutes

1. Give each student a card and explain that she or he should write a sentence to encourage someone or to show friendship and caring to another.

2. Collect the cards, shuffle them, and redistribute them. Ask students to read their cards aloud.

Discussion

1. Which of the statements do you feel we do best as a class? Which statement seems to be hardest for our class?

2. How might we encourage each other to be more caring?

Journal

1. What does the saying "A chain is only as strong as the weakest link" mean?

2. If someone tried to help you become a more caring person, would you feel threatened?

Four of a Kind

Multiple Intelligence: Verbal/Linguistic   **Grade: 3 and Up**
Life Habit: Organization   **Time: 15 to 20 minutes**
Materials: Paper and pencils, plus a copy of the diagram (Figure 1.1) for each group

1. Form the students into groups of 4. Students should sit with one on each side of the diagram and write their names on that side of the diagram.

2. Ask groups to talk briefly to discover four things they all agree they like or dislike. This must be unanimous. Groups should write their four choices in the inner squares of the diagram.

3. Ask students to agree on four things or ways in which they are different. For example, one student may have four sisters, another may like buttermilk, and so on. Ask students to write their differences on the side panels of the diagram.

4. Ask each group to present their diagram to the class.

Discussion

1. What did this activity show you?

2. What surprised you in your group?

3. Was it easier to find something you all agreed you liked or disliked or to find ways you were different?

FIGURE 1.1. Four of a Kind Diagram

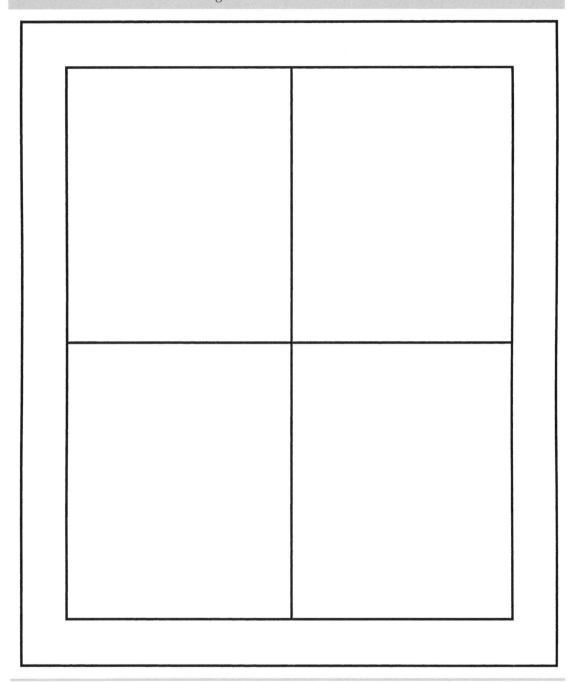

1. What would it be like if everyone in the world liked the same things?   **Journal**

2. What would the world be like if everyone were exactly the same?

Team Name Puzzle

Multiple Intelligence: Verbal/Linguistic **Grade: 3 and Up**
Life Habit: Organization **Time: 15 to 20 minutes**
Materials: Large paper, whiteboard, or chalkboard; markers

1. This activity involves the whole class. You may wish to divide the class into groups of 5 or 6 at first, and then try the larger class group.

2. Explain that the object of this game is to connect the first name of each member of the group in a crostic puzzle (see Figure 1.2).

3. Ask one student to begin by printing his or her name on the paper or board. Then, one by one, students connect their names to those already printed. Students are more successful if they carefully watch the puzzle develop, make suggestions, and listen.

Discussion
1. What was the most difficult part of this activity? What would have helped make this easier?

2. What happened when you got stuck?

Journal
1. Have you read or heard any news stories about an activity or event in which people have to figure out how to reach a goal that seems impossible? Describe it.

2. Is there any situation at school that requires people to put together people or things that don't seem to fit? Describe it.

FIGURE 1.2. Team Name Puzzle

```
                    E
                    R
                    I               E
          T     C A R O L
      B R I A             A
          A               I
          C               N
          Y               E
```

Pig Latin Review

Multiple Intelligence: Verbal/Linguistic   **Grade: 3 and Up**
Life Habit: Confidence   **Time: 30 minutes**
Materials: None

1. Before beginning, make sure students know how to speak in Pig Latin. The first sound of a word is dropped and added to the end of the word with an "ay" sound (e.g., eskday = desk; ouyay = you; estionquay = question).

2. Choose material recently studied by the class. Tell students you are going to review this unit. Select or ask for two volunteers to serve as expert and interpreter.

3. As the review begins, students ask questions about the material studied. The "interpreter" translates the question into Pig Latin and the "expert" answers in Pig Latin. The "interpreter" then gives the answer in English to the class.

4. After a certain number of questions, switch expert and interpreter.

1. Set up a panel of "experts" with a Pig Latin interpreter.   **Variations**

2. Have a Pig Latin discussion between two "experts" with an interpreter.

3. Hold class in Pig Latin.

4. Let the class make up another language pattern and use it in a review activity.

How did you feel as you listened to the Pig Latin review?   **Discussion**

In your own "nonsense" language, write five simple questions and answers.   **Journal**

2 Mathematical/Logical Intelligence

Children with mathematical and logical intelligence think conceptually. They like to explore patterns, categories, and relations, and continually ask questions about the world around them. They like puzzles and games requiring reasoning abilities. They are frequently found in the company of a computer or a chemistry set.

Look for children who easily solve mental math problems and enjoy using math skills; ask questions about such things as the beginning of the universe, or what happens after death; play and win checkers and chess; and work patiently on experiments and puzzles.

To nurture Mathematical/Logical Intelligence, encourage the use of experiments and their data records, logic puzzles, graphs, charts, diagrams, geometric designs, comparisons, analysis, contrasts, prediction, story grids, classifications, and Venn diagrams, among other projects.

Skyscraper

Multiple Intelligence: Mathematical/Logical	**Grade: 2 and Up**
Life Habit: Cooperation	**Time: 45 minutes**
Materials: Newspaper, roll of tape per team	

1. Divide the class into groups of 4. Pass out newspaper and a roll of tape to each group.

2. Instruct groups that they are to try make the tallest free-standing structure they can out of the newspaper. They have 10 minutes to plan how to do this and 15 minutes to construct the skyscraper. During the construction time, there is NO TALKING. Groups have to communicate nonverbally.

3. During the planning period, circulate among the groups and make sure everyone understands the activity. Call "Time" after 10 minutes.

4. Allow 15 minutes for construction. Circulate among the groups.

1. Was your team successful? Why or why not?   **Discussion**

2. What would you do differently if you were to do this again?

1. Did you feel able to communicate your ideas to the rest of the group, or did you feel overpowered by another's quick actions? How could you have communicated more clearly?   **Journal**

2. Have you ever been in a situation where each person wanted his plan followed and refused to consider other ideas? Describe what happened.

Geometeam

Multiple Intelligence: Mathematical/Logical   **Grade: 5 and Up**
Life Habit: Cooperation   **Time: 20 minutes**
Materials: 15-foot piece of rope or heavy string; blindfold for each member of group

1. This is a whole class activity. Arrange the rope in a circle. Ask the team to stand in a circle around the rope.

2. Tell the students to discuss the different kinds of polygons they might make with the rope and then agree on one figure they will make. They have 5 minutes to do this.

3. Then give the team blindfolds and explain that they must make the polygon figure they chose while wearing the blindfolds.

This can be done with two groups. Have one group do the activity while the second group observes. Then let the second group perform the activity while the first group observes.   **Variation**

1. How did your team decide which figure to make?   **Discussion**

2. How did your team members communicate with one another when they were unable to see one another? Was one person "in charge"? Who had trouble?

3. What Life Habits did you use to solve this problem?

Journal   What would happen if each person in the group had a different idea of the shape to make? Describe the scene, including dialogue.

Pretzel Puzzle

Multiple Intelligence: Mathematical/Logical   Grade: K and Up
Life Habit: Initiative   Time: 30 minutes
Materials: None

1. Form groups of 10 to 15 students each. One person from each group is chosen to leave the room. The remaining students hold hands and form a circle.

2. Once the circle is formed, tell students to tangle themselves up as much as possible by going through each other's arms, under legs, and so on. Tell them not to let go of each other's hands.

3. Once students are tangled and "twisted," the person sent out of the room is called back and tries to get the circle back to its original state.

Discussion   1. Were there people in your group who took the initiative to help out when everything seemed confused?

2. How many wanted to give up before you got untangled?

3. How did it feel once you were all untangled?

Journal   1. Did you want to offer advice but decided not to? Why?

2. Have there been times when you could have taken the initiative to help out in a situation, but you didn't? Do you think it would have turned out differently if you had helped?

Saving for a Rainy Day

Multiple Intelligence: Mathematical/Logical   Grade: 5 and Up
Life Habit: Responsibility   Time: 15 to 30 minutes
Materials: Calculator and/or paper and pencils for each pair of
    students, blackboard or overhead projector

1. Arrange students in pairs. Tell students they are making a choice about the best method of saving money.

2. Using the board or an overhead projector, present these two choices for saving money:

a. Save $1,000 a day every day during the month of September (Total saved: $30,000).

b. Start by saving one cent on the first day and then double the amount each day during the month of June (one cent the first day, two cents the second day, four cents the third day, eight cents the fourth day)(Total saved: $5,368,708.80).

3. Ask the students to discuss these choices and decide the best way to save money during a 30-day period. Allow about three minutes for this.

4. Distribute calculators and ask students to figure how much they would save with the method they chose. Then they should calculate the results based on the other method of saving.

1. How did you and your partner arrive at a decision? **Discussion**

2. Were you surprised at the results of your calculations? Why?

Make a list of dos and don'ts of saving money for a family of five. **Journal**

Let's Have a Party!

Multiple Intelligence: Mathematical/Logical **Grade: 3 and Up**
Life Habit: Motivation **Time: 45 minutes**
Materials: For each group "assembly line"—supplies and a
  5″ × 8″ index card with their directions on it (see Figure 2.1).

1. First, distribute the supplies randomly among six grocery bags, so that all of one group's materials are not in one bag. Place the bags at various places in the room. Provide a working surface for all six groups, a place for students to wash their hands, and a serving area.

2. Explain to students that this activity is a long one. To be successful, each group has to follow directions and perform the tasks as they are given on the group's card.

3. Tell them all the materials they need for their part of the party preparation are in the grocery bags around the room. Part of their job is to gather their materials. There is no talking once the activity begins.

4. Divide the students into six groups. Before giving out the cards, ask if there are any questions. Distribute the cards and start the groups on their tasks.

Discussion   1. How motivated were you to find your supplies? Why?

2. If your homework assignments had been in the bags, would you have looked for them in a different way? What does this tell you about motivation?

Journal   What did you enjoy most about the party?

FIGURE 2.1. Cards for "Let's Have a Party"

Group I: Oranges

You will be making orange sections for 28 people. You'll need:

7 oranges   4 plastic bags

2 knives   paper towels

When you get all this together, follow these steps:

1. Wash your hands.
2. Wash the oranges.
3. Wipe them dry.
4. Cut each orange into four equal pieces.
5. Place the orange pieces into the plastic bags.
6. Put the bags on the serving table.
7. Clean up your workstation.
8. Wash your hands.

When you're finished, return your card and wait quietly for the other groups to finish.

Group II: Celery

You will be making celery sticks for 28 people. You'll need:

celery   2 knives   4 plastic bags

When you have everything on your list, begin.

1. Wash your hands.
2. Wash the celery.
3. Cut the celery into small sticks.
4. Divide the celery sticks among the 4 bags.
5. Place the bags on the serving table.
6. Clean up your workstation.
7. Wash your hands.

When you have finished everything, please wait quietly until the others have finished.

FIGURE 2.1. Continued

Group III: Cracker Sandwiches

You will make peanut butter cracker sandwiches for 28 people. You'll need:

crackers   peanut butter

3 table knives   28 plates

When you have gathered everything you need, begin.

1. Wash your hands.
2. Count out 28 crackers.
3. Spread each cracker with peanut butter.
4. Put a second cracker on top to make a sandwich.
5. Put one sandwich on each plate.
6. Place the plates on the serving table.
7. Clean up your area.
8. Wash your hands.

When you are finished, return the card. Wait quietly for the rest of the class to finish.

Group IV: Cheese

You will be making cheese cubes for 28 people. You'll need:

cheese   2 table knives   4 plastic bags

When you have everything you need, begin.

1. Wash your hands.
2. Cut the cheese into 28 cubes.
3. Put the cheese cubes in the 4 plastic bags.
4. Clean up your work station.
5. Wash your hands.

When you have finished everything, return this card, and wait quietly for the others to finish.

(continued)

FIGURE 2.1. Continued

Group V: Lemonade

You will make enough lemonade to fill a gallon container. You'll need:

2 cans frozen lemonade concentrate   gallon container

spoon   28 cups

small plastic pouring pitcher

When you have all these items, begin.

1. Wash your hands.
2. Follow the directions for mixing the lemonade.
3. When you have finished, use the small pitcher to pour the 28 cups of lemonade.
4. Clean up your workstation.
5. Wash your hands.

When you have finished everything, return this card and wait quietly for the others to finish.

Group VI: Apples

You will be making apple slices for 28 people. You'll need:

7 apples   2 knives   4 plastic bags

When you have gathered all these, begin.

1. Wash your hands.
2. Wash the apples.
3. Cut each apple into four slices.
4. Cut out the seeds.
5. Place the slices in the plastic bags.
6. Put the bags on the serving table.
7. Clean up your area.
8. Wash your hands.

When you're finished, hand in your card and wait quietly for others to finish.

Pass the Number, Please

Multiple Intelligence: Mathematical/Logical	**Grade: 5 and Up**
Life Habit: Alertness	**Time: 10 to 15 minutes**
Materials: None	

1. Ask students to sit in a circle. Explain that they will work with numbers in a pattern determined by them; one person says a number; the next repeats that number and adds a second one in the sequence of his or her choice; the third player repeats the first two numbers and adds a third in the sequence. Play continues around the circle.

2. When a player forgets the sequence or leaves out a number, he or she is out.

3. When it seems that the players have caught on to the sequence, a player may change it. This player must make it clear what the new sequence is. Otherwise, both this player and the next player are out. If you wish, you may allow the new sequence to be announced. The player may shout "Change!" before beginning a new sequence.

4. Play a round for 5 minutes or so. Then play a second round.

Example

2 4 6 8 10 12 (change) 13 14 15 16 17 18 (change) 20 22 24, and so on.

Discussion

1. Focus on the moments of change. How did you feel when making the change?

2. Did you feel sure the group would understand the direction in which you were leading them?

3. How did you feel when the next person failed to see the new sequence?

4. How did you feel when you were the second person and went out?

Journal

List occupations in which alertness to change can be very important. Choose one occupation from your list and explain the reasons for your choice.

High Card Wins!

Multiple Intelligences: Mathematical/Logical	**Grade: 1 and Up**
Life Habit: Alertness	**Time: 15 minutes**
Materials: Deck of playing cards with the face cards, jokers, and aces removed	

Give all the following directions before distributing cards to students.

1. Tell the students that they are going to play a card game in which they have to notice other people and act according to the card others hold on their foreheads. Explain that each student receives a card,

face down. They are not to look at their cards until the very end of the game.

2. Explain that only numbered cards are used and that a high card (8,9,10) means that a person is important or popular. A low card (2,3,4) means the person is not very important and unpopular. The rest (5,6,7) are in the middle.

3. Explain that when you give the signal, they are to pick up their cards, not looking at the face side, and hold the cards to their foreheads so that the card's face is showing. (Demonstrate to be sure everyone understands.)

4. Players should then walk around the classroom, treating people with high numbers as if they are important and popular, people with low numbers as if they are not important or popular. They may not tell other students what their numbers are or use glasses or mirrors to see their own numbers. This activity only works when no one knows his or her own number and is simply reacting to the others' numbers.

5. Allow students to follow these directions and mill around the room for 5 minutes. Tell them to line up in order from 2 to 10, placing themselves where they think they should fit in the lineup. Their decision should be based on how they were treated by others. They should still be unaware of the actual numbers on their cards.

6. Finally, direct students to look at their cards.

Discussion

1. How did you decide what number you were? What behaviors gave you clues?

2. Encourage high, middle, and low numbers to talk about behavior clues they received.

Journal

1. Once you had clues about your number, did it affect how you treated other students with different numbers? If you felt you were a high number, did you behave differently toward those with low numbers? Why or why not?

2. What life lessons does this activity teach?

What Should We Buy?

Multiple Intelligence: Mathematical/Logical　　　　**Grade: 3 and Up**
Life Habit: Integrity　　　　**Time: 5 to 10 minutes**
Materials: One catalog or advertising section from Sunday's paper for each pair, paper, pens or pencils.

1. Pair up the students. Explain that each pair will have a catalog from which to choose three items that they agree they like best. Distribute

the catalogs. After they have agreed, ask the students to write down their choices and list reasons for their choices.

2. If there is time, ask some of the pairs to share their choices and reasons.

1. You might ask students to choose three items that are the most useful—or most important.

2. For older students, you might make cards assigning each pair a specific lifestyle, occupation, income, size of family, ages of family members, and so on.

1. Was it easy to arrive at a decision together? What made it easy?

2. What problems did you have as you tried to reach an agreement?

1. Do you think that the average person carefully thinks through purchases before buying? Why or why not? In your opinion, is it important to do so?

2. Did you feel pressured to agree with your partner? Explain.

My Circle of Circles

Multiple Intelligence: Mathematical/Logical **Grade: 2 and Up**
Life Habit: Self-Awareness **Time: 10 to 15 minutes**
Materials: Blackboard, worksheet (see Figure 2.2), and writing tool

1. Give each student a "Circle of Circles" worksheet. Ask students to write their names in the middle circle.

2. In the surrounding circles, each student should write words describing places or groups to which they feel connected. Examples include church, school, friends, family, scouts, sports teams, and so on.

3. When students are finished, name some common groups or places, and ask students to stand if they listed the word in one of their circles. Each time a word is given, ask a student to list the word on the board and count the number of students who listed it. Ask a different student for each word, if you wish. You may graph the number of responses if you wish to work on graphing skills.

4. Then, ask if any students would like to share something that wasn't named. As a student names a word, ask others to stand if they had that word in one of their circles.

1. Were you surprised at how many or how few students listed the same things as you? Why?

2. What are the benefits of belonging to a group?

3. How do groups usually form?

4. Are there groups that have negative influences? Can a group with a positive focus unintentionally hurt others?

Journal

1. Is there a benefit in knowing others share the same connections as you? If so, what is that benefit?

2. What would the world be like if everyone had different interests and different ways of connecting?

FIGURE 2.2. Circle of Circles

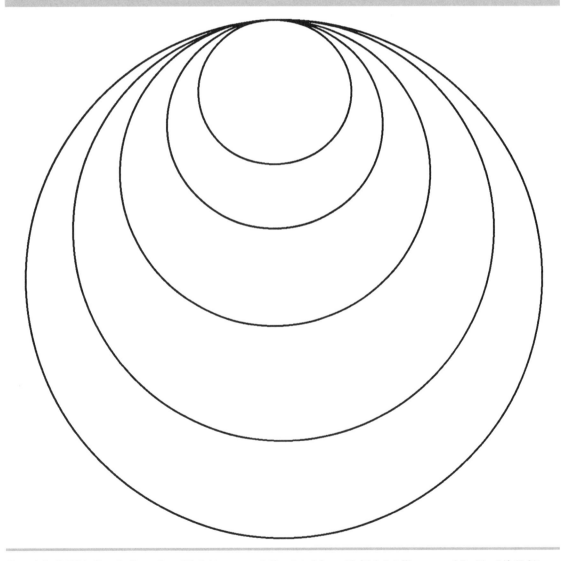

What's Bugging You?

Multiple Intelligence: Mathematical/Logical   **Grade: K and Up**
Life Habit: Self-Awareness   **Time: 10 to 15 minutes**
Materials: Chalkboard for recording answers

1. Begin by asking students what it means to be "bugged" about something. How does it feel? How do you feel about people who do things that bug you?

2. Ask the students to name things that "bug" them and list them on the board. When this process seems done, ask the students to select the most "bugging" things on the list. Then read the list, one item at a time, and ask students to raise their hands or stand up to indicate if an item was on their lists. Student assistants can help tally the votes.

3. Circle the five "top bugs." An extension activity might be individual pledges to avoid these five bugs in the classroom.

1. Were you surprised at the five "top bugs"?   **Discussion**

2. If someone is doing one of the top five "bugs," what would you do?

3. Why is it helpful to know what bugs someone else?

1. Is it possible to do something that bugs someone else but seems perfectly normal and okay to you? Give an example and explain.   **Journal**

2. Do you think any "bugs" on your list should have been on the top five? Why?

Coop Squares

Multiple Intelligence: Mathematical/Logical   **Grade: 5 and Up**
Life Habit: Patience   **Time: 15 minutes**
Materials: Copy of the squares (Figure 2.3) for each group

1. Divide the class into groups of 3 or 4 students each. Distribute a copy of the squares to each group.

2. Have the groups determine the number of perfect squares they can find in the handout.

3. Give the groups 5 minutes to count as many squares as possible (40 is the maximum number of squares).

4. Give groups an opportunity to share with others the number of squares they found. They probably have differing answers. Allow them to go back and count again.

Discussion

1. How did your group go about working on the problem?

2. Did anyone in your group become frustrated? How did your group handle this?

3. How did you feel after the first count? the second count?

Journal

It was important to be patient while working on this puzzle. Describe another situation in which patience is very important. Give reasons for your choice.

FIGURE 2.3. Coop Squares

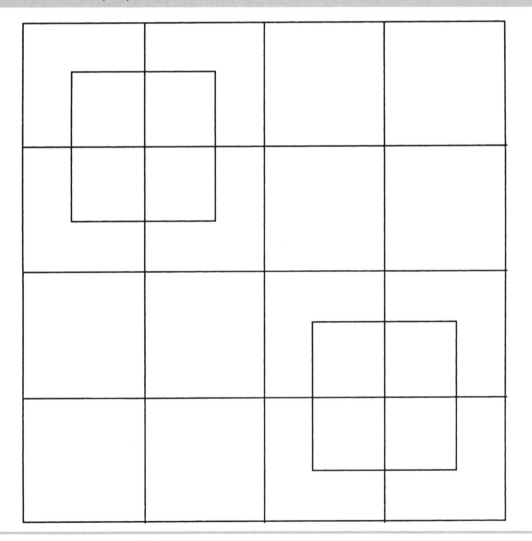

Class-O-Graph

Multiple Intelligence: Mathematical/Logical   **Grade: 3 and Up**

Life Habit: Curiosity   **Time: Two sessions of 15 to 30 minutes each**

Materials: List of the names of all the students in the class, a sheet of graph paper for each student, pens or pencils

1. Ask students to name characteristics that distinguish one person from another—other than physical appearance. Write their suggestions on the board. These may include size of family, favorite sport, and so on. Then, ask students to choose one characteristic that they would like to find out about their classmates.

2. Give each student a copy of the class list. Students should ask their classmates how they fit into the category and then record the answers on their class lists. Collect the papers.

Return papers to the students with a sheet of graph paper and ask them to graph what they learned from their survey.

Session A

Session B

Note: This activity may be used in many ways. Younger students may simply list the number of students who gave the same answer, or their task may be simplified into asking an "either-or" question. Instead of graphing, older students may be asked to do a fraction or decimal analysis of their data.

Bean Jar

Multiple Intelligence: Mathematical/Logical   **Grade: 4 and Up**

Life Habit: Confidence   **Time: 40 to 50 minutes**

Materials: A jar filled with beans that have previously been counted

1. Set the jar of beans in a place where everyone can see it. Tell everyone to make an individual estimate of the number of beans in the jar. Record the estimates in a column on the board.

2. Group students in pairs.

3. Ask each pair to make an estimate. Record the results on the board.

4. Group the pairs into quartets. Repeat the process in Step 3.

5. Group the quartets into octets. Repeat the process in Step 3.

Discussion
1. How did you feel during each decision-making process—alone, in pairs, fours, eights?

2. How did your feelings change? Which was most comfortable for you?

Journal
Why do people sometimes change their personal opinions when they are in a large group? Describe a situation in which such a change might be for the best.

Going Once, Going Twice, Sold!

Multiple Intelligence: Mathematical/Logical   **Grade: 4 and Up**
Life Habit: Confidence   **Time: 45 minutes**
Materials: Play money (Figure 2.4), copy of Life Habits

1. Divide the class into groups of 4 or 5 students each. Tell students you are going to auction off the Life Habits to the highest bidder (see the Life Habits chart in the Introduction).

2. Give each team $1,000 to buy different Life Habits. The $1,000 packets should be made up of various denominations.

3. Ask for a volunteer to be the auctioneer.

4. Before the auction begins, give the groups time to decide the Habits of most value to them. They should also determine the highest dollar amount they will pay for each. Point out that the more Life Habits they have, the better they are prepared for life.

5. Begin the auction, one Life Habit at a time.

Discussion
1. Which Life Habits sold for the greatest amount? Do you feel that these are indeed the most important ones?

2. Chart your team's top four choices made before the auction. What does the chart tell you? How does it compare with what you actually bought?

Journal
1. Did you agree with your team's first choice? Why or why not?

2. Choose another Life Habit and explain why you feel it is important.

FIGURE 2.4. Going Once, Twice, Sold

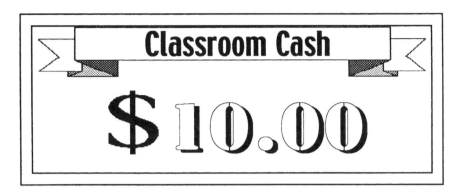

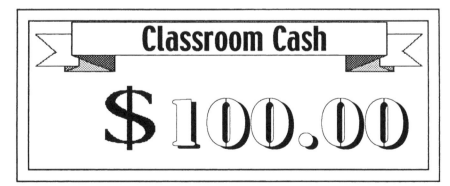

Balloon Castle

Multiple Intelligence: Mathematical/Logical   **Grade: 6 and Up**
Life Habit: Organization   **Time: 30 to 60 minutes,
including planning time**
**Materials: 2 rolls of transparent tape per team and 100 balloons
(or as many as time and budget allow)**

1. Give the materials to each team of 5 to 12 students and explain that the objective is to build the tallest, freestanding, self-supporting balloon structure possible in 20 minutes. Allow 10 minutes for team planning.

2. Announce that the teams are to begin. Once they start, there should be no talking. Call "Time" after 20 minutes.

Discussion

1. How did your team arrive at your first plan for a balloon castle?

2. Did it work out as planned? If not, how did you decide what changes were needed?

3. What problems did you have as you built?

Journal   Would this be easier if you did it on your own? Why or why not?

The House

Multiple Intelligence: Mathematical/Logical   **Grade: 4 and Up**
Life Habit: Organization   **Time: 30 to 40 minutes**
Materials: 30- to 40-foot piece of rope or heavy yarn

1. Tell the members of the team (the whole class) to take hold of the rope. Their task is to form a house shape with the roofline (or envelope shape) without the rope doubling back on itself.

2. They may not let go of the rope or trade places, but they may slide their hands along the rope.

Discussion

1. How many different ideas did the group have? How did you decide what to try first?

2. What made this activity difficult to achieve?

3. If one rule were changed, which would be the best one to change?

Journal

1. How did you feel as the group tried to make the figure?

2. Is there anything in real life that is like this exercise? What? How?

3 Visual/Spatial Intelligence

Children gifted in this intelligence seem to know where everything is located in the classroom. They think in three-dimensional pictures rather than words and have the ability to see, remember, and recreate an object. They are sensitive to changes in their physical environment and like to design, build, and invent. This intelligence is usually accompanied by a strong imagination.

Look for children who do artwork whenever possible; doodle; daydream; relate seeing clear mental pictures of people, places and things; easily read maps, charts, and diagrams; work visual puzzles and mazes; enjoy art and visual presentations.

To nurture Verbal/Linguistic Intelligence, encourage viewing and creating movies, book covers, cartoons and comic strips, scrapbooks, bulletin boards, 3-D diagrams and models, masks, costumes, displays, dioramas, family trees, filmstrips, game boards, maps, stained glass, models, murals, exhibits, bumper stickers, and flip books, among others.

Build a Better Bike

Multiple Intelligence: Visual/Spatial　　　　**Grade: K and Up**
Life Habit: Creativity　　　　**Time: 20 minutes**
Materials: Paper and pencil

1. Organize the class into groups of 6 to 8 students. Ask each group to appoint a recorder (with K-2 children, use an older student or adult helper)

2. Remind the class to use the DOVE rule for brainstorming:

   ◆ D stands for Defer judgment
   ◆ O stands for Original ideas

- ◆ V stand for Vast number
- ◆ E stands for Expand and elaborate

3. Groups have 5 minutes to call out and write down as many ideas as possible in response to the question:

How could we design a better bicycle, one that is more enjoyable, efficient, and comfortable than ordinary, everyday bikes?

4. Stop the groups after 5 minutes and have the recorder read the list to the class. Encourage applause after each report.

Variation Groups could also draw a picture of their bike design.

Discussion
1. Are many heads better than one for this kind of activity?

2. What would have happened if your group had stopped to judge or discuss each idea?

3. What are some other ways brainstorming could be used?

Journal
1. Can something that seems like a silly idea become something useful? Give an example.

2. Was it hard not to judge other people's suggestions? Why or why not?

Creature Stew

Multiple Intelligence: Visual/Spatial   **Grade: 4 and Up**
Life Habit: Creativity   **Time: 30 Minutes**
Materials: Drawing materials

1. Divide the class into teams of 3 or 4 students each. Ask each team to choose one of the Life Habits.

2. Ask the teams to discuss and list the characteristics of their specific Life Habit.

3. Direct the students to think of characteristics they can use in creating a creature with their Life Habit. For example, a creature with perseverance may have antennae to keep it tuned in at all times. It may have a cheetah's strong legs to run quickly in the right direction and a cable car's cable to keep it on the right track.

4. Ask each team to create a picture of their creature that shows the physical attributes of its Life Habit.

1. Ask each team to tell the class which Life Habit they chose and explain why they designed their creature as they did. Allow time for discussion. **Discussion**

2. Was there anything about your Life Habit creature that you couldn't show? If so, ask the class for suggestions.

Choose another Life Habit, create a creature, and write a story that shows its characteristics. **Journal**

Space Invention

Multiple Intelligence: Visual/Spatial   **Grade: 2 and Up**
Life Habit: Creativity   **Time: 5 minutes for each group**
Materials: Set of objects (example: 6 chairs, 3 books, 1 small shoe-size box), one index card for each group

1. Arrange the students in groups of 5. Explain that each group will use the assigned set of objects to create an environment or setting in the classroom. They may also use themselves as part of the set. They do not have to use all the objects, but they may not add other objects to their set.

2. Give the first group a card that names a setting. They have 5 minutes to create the setting. Then, the rest of the class guesses what they have created.

3. Move to the second group, then the third, and so on.

A boat, a church, a bank, a bus, a movie theatre, an island, a mall **Setting Suggestions**

1. What did you like about this activity? **Discussion**

2. Was your setting difficult to create with the objects?

3. Which setting do you think was the easiest to create? Why or why not? Does the group that created what you consider to be the easiest set agree? Why or why not?

How was this exercise like cooking without a recipe? What other activity is similar? Explain. **Journal**

Motto Making

Multiple Intelligence: Visual/Spatial　　　　　**Grade: 3 and Up**

Life Habit: Creativity

Time: 45 to 60 minutes if students do the research; 20 to 30 minutes if cards with flags and mottoes are premade

Materials: Almanacs or other reference materials with state and/or national flags and mottoes; 3″ × 5″ cards; construction paper or poster board; markers or crayons (or, before the activity, glue photocopies of flags and mottoes onto 3″ × 5″ cards)

1. Divide the class into groups of 4 or 5 students each, or, if students are already divided into working groups, use those groups. This could also be used as a whole class project.

2. Explain that the purpose of activity is to design a flag and motto for the group.

3. After looking at and thinking about the flags and mottoes of each of the United States and/or nations of the world, groups should agree on a design and motto for themselves.

Discussion
1. Did you divide the labor? How was that decided? Was everyone in agreement?

2. What is your favorite part of your design/motto?

Journal
Design a motto and a flag to represent you personally. Give reasons for your choices.

Building With Cards

Multiple Intelligence: Visual/Spatial　　　　　**Grade: 2 and Up**

Life Habit: Patience　　　　　**Time: 10 to 15 minutes**

Materials: One deck (or another equal number) of cards for each group of 3 students

1. Divide students into groups of 3. Give each group a deck (or another equal number) of cards. (Cards need not form an actual playing deck.)

2. Ask the students to build a three-story building using only the cards.

3. As the students work, watch for signs of anger or frustration. If the frustration level gets too high, end the activity, or end it after about 10 minutes, unless everyone seems occupied and focused.

1. What did you think when you heard the task described? **Discussion**

2. How did you feel when you first started?

3. After you had tried and failed a few times, how did you feel? How did your group feel? How did your group handle anger, discouragement, or frustration?

What situations or activities frustrate you or make you angry? What do you do to handle your negative feelings? What other things could you do? **Journal**

Cats 'n' Dogs

Multiple Intelligence: Visual/Spatial   **Grade: K and Up**
Life Habits: Fair Play   **Time: 45 minutes**
Materials: Drawing materials

1. Discuss the meaning of conflict. Have students cite examples from their lives. Also look at national and international conflicts past and present.

2. Have students draw pictures to show how to keep a dog and cat from fighting.

3. Ask for volunteers to share their pictures. Call attention to the different solutions that students developed.

1. When applying the cat-dog solutions to humans, are there any solutions that would be appropriate without making any changes? Why? Are there any cat-dog solutions that would not work with humans? Why? **Discussion**

2. How could these solutions be applied on a larger scale to group, national, or international conflicts?

3. Can you think of solutions that haven't been discussed? What are they?

1. Have you used any of the solutions discussed today to deal with your personal conflicts? Which ones? How successful were they? **Journal**

2. Name a solution discussed today that you like. Please explain why.

TABLE 3.1   List for Symbol Silhouette

1. The top of the head—things we think about

2. The eyes—things we like to see or watch

3. The ears—what we like to hear or listen to

4. The mouth—what we like to talk about

5. The stomach—what we like to eat

6. The heart—what we feel strongly about

7. The shoulders—problems we must face

8. The right hand—things we like to make

9. The left hand—things we like to play or do

10. The right thigh—colors we like to wear

11. The left thigh—our fears or worries

12. The right foot—places we have been

13. The left foot—places we would like to go

Symbol Silhouette

Multiple Intelligence: Visual/Spatial   **Grade: 5 and Up**

Life Habit: Cooperation   **Time: 45 to 60 minutes**

Materials: Sheet of paper large enough to draw a body outline of one student (one sheet per group), markers, scissors, magazines, glue, blackboard or flip chart

1. Arrange students in groups of 4 to 6. Explain that they will create a group profile (see Table 3.1) on a silhouette.

2. Next each group chooses a member to lie down on the large paper and traces an outline of the chosen person.

3. Give each group a copy of the List for Symbol Silhouette (Table 3.1) or display them on the board, a flip chart, or by other means. Each part of the silhouette represents something agreed upon by the group and then indicated on the silhouette.

4. When the silhouettes are finished, each group should select a spokesperson to explain the group silhouette to the other groups. Then the silhouettes can be displayed with the names of each group member. Silhouettes may be simple outlines or "dressed."

1. How did you decide what would go in each part of the silhouette?

Discussion

2. Which part was the most difficult to agree upon?

3. In what way or ways is your group's silhouette different from the other groups' silhouettes?

1. How do you feel when people talk about the "normal" or the "typi-cal" student or teenager? Write a description of the "normal" or "typical" adult from your point of view.

Journal

2. How would the world change if we never thought of people in groups, but always as individuals?

Partner Drawing

Multiple Intelligence: Visual/Spatial   **Grade: 5 and Up**
Life Habit: Cooperation   **Time: 5 to 10 minutes**
Materials: Plain white paper, one crayon for each student

1. Divide students into pairs. They will be drawing together. Ask each student to choose one crayon. Tell pairs to place the paper on the table between them.

2. Explain that they will be given a category and, without talking, they will take turns drawing an example of the category one stroke at a time. Keep the categories general enough so the students have some flexibility in choosing what to draw. Allow 5 minutes for this activity.

3. Create a gallery of the drawings.

The category is flowers. The first student has a yellow crayon, the second has a red one. The first student makes one long straight line. The second student draws a curve out from the middle of the line. The first student decides this could be the beginning of a leaf and connects it with another curved line going back to the straight line. This continues.

Example

Discussion
1. How did you and your partner manage to work without using words?

2. Did you enjoy this activity? Were you and your partner surprised at your finished drawing? How was it different from what you each had in mind at the beginning?

Journal
1. Imagine a gallery of partner drawings. Describe one.

2. Make up a short biography for each artist and tell how they happened to work together.

Chain of Links

Multiple Intelligence: Visual/Spatial　　　　**Grade: 2 and Up**
Life Habit: Motivation　　　　**Time: 2 to 3 minutes throughout the class; ongoing**
Materials: Strips of construction paper, 1 inch wide by 9 inches long; glue or tape; markers

1. Put a basket or plastic container of the strips of construction paper on a desk or table where all of the students have access to it. Each time a student reaches a goal, the student records the goal on a strip, along with his or her name, and adds the strip to the chain of strips being formed by the class.

2. As the chain grows, hang it around the room so students can see their group progress.

The Power Chair

Multiple Intelligence: Visual/Spatial　　　　**Grade: 3 and Up**
Life Habit: Courage　　　　**Time: 10 to 20 minutes**
Materials: 6 chairs

1. Arrange the students in a circle around the chairs. Explain that this activity has to do with power. Call for volunteers to come to the center of the circle and arrange the chairs so it is clear which chair has the power or is in control of the rest of the chairs.

2. Do this as many times as the students have ideas about arranging the chairs so it is obvious one chair has power over the others.

3. When the last arrangement has been made, ask if someone would like to sit in the chair of power. When that student is seated, ask if someone else has an idea of a way to move into a more powerful position than the person in the power chair. Chairs may still be moved, but the person in the power chair must stay in place.

4. Do this as many times as the students have ideas.

Discussion

1. Where was the power chair usually placed? Why?

2. How did it feel to be in the power chair?

3. How did it feel to move things around so that you changed the power position?

4. Do people try to move into power positions when they interact? Is that good or bad?

Journal

1. Think of a way for everyone in a group or situation to have power. Describe in detail.

2. Does it take courage to move into a position of power? Why or why not?

It's Like . . .

Multiple Intelligence: Visual/Spatial　　　　**Grade: 3 and Up**
Life Habit: Initiative　　　　　　　　　　**Time: 45 minutes**
Materials: Copy paper, colored pencils, blackboard

1. Choose four or five Life Habits and write them on the board. They may relate to specific problems the class is having.

2. Divide the class into teams of 4 or 5 students and ask them to choose one Life Habit their group would like to explore. Tell them to list five or six words describing this Life Habit.

3. When they finish, ask them to decide what musical instrument, food, game, and animal would best describe the Life Habit. Ask each team to fold a sheet of paper into four equal sections and write Instrument, Food, Game, or Animal in each section and draw a picture of that item in that section of the paper.

4. Teams should share their charts and discuss the reasons for their choices.

Discussion

1. How did your group decide on the Life Habit?

2. What was the most difficult section of the chart to decide upon? Why?

3. How did you decide what to draw?

Journal

1. Using the same Life Habit, draw a geometric design to represent it.

2. Choose another Life Habit, write a description of it, and draw a doodle to represent it.

Friendly Web

Multiple Intelligence: Visual/Spatial   **Grade: 1 and Up**
Life Habit: Perseverance/Effort   **Time: 10 minutes**
Materials: Large ball of yarn

1. Ask the class to stand in a circle. Call for a volunteer to stand in the center.

2. Tell the class that they will be creating a maze around the person in the circle.

3. Give the ball of yarn to one player in the circle. The person holding the ball must hold on to one end of the yarn and then pass the ball to another player in the circle.

4. Players should follow these three rules:

   ◆ The yarn ball must be passed from one player to the next without directly crossing over the person in the center.

   ◆ The ball cannot be passed directly to either the right or the left of the person with the yarn.

   ◆ The one passing the yarn must hold a section of the yarn when passing the ball.

5. After about 3 minutes of making the maze, ask the players to undo the maze by passing the ball back in the order in which it was passed. The person in the center helps those in the circle figure out how to pass the ball.

Discussion   Was your class successful? How did it feel as you were creating the web? What did you need to untangle it?

Journal   Write about a time in your life when it was important to persevere. Be sure to explain how the Life Habit of perseverance helped you.

Building a Shelter

Multiple Intelligence: Visual/Spatial   **Grade: 5 and Up**
Life Habit: Organization   **Time: 45 to 60 minutes**
**Materials: For each group—paper grocery sack filled with news-
    papers and one roll of masking tape**

1. Divide the class into groups of 4 or 5 students. Explain that each group will receive one roll of tape and one bag of newspapers to use

to build a shelter. The shelter should be able to stand by itself and all the students in the group should fit in the shelter. It can be taped only to itself and the floor.

2. The group has 5 minutes to plan how to accomplish this task and assign jobs to each member. At the end of 5 minutes, they are not allowed to speak and must communicate nonverbally. (During the building phase, circulate from group to group and speak to groups that seem to be having difficulty. Remind the students that this is a cooperative activity and everyone should participate.)

3. If time is running out, you may reduce the structure to the size of a doghouse.

Discussion

1. What strategies did you use to make decisions and work together?

2. What was the most difficult part of the task? What was easy?

3. How did you manage to overcome the problems that occurred?

Journal

1. Would you rather do this kind of activity alone or with a group of people? Explain your answer.

2. Describe in detail the shelter your group built. Give the structure a name that fits the group of people who built it.

Claymotion

Multiple Intelligence: Visual/Spatial **Grade: K and Up**
Life Habit: Communication **Time: 45 minutes**
Materials: A small amount of sculpting clay for each pair of students

1. Place students in pairs. Have one student in each pair write down or whisper to the partner an emotion he or she has felt. The partner then tries to use the clay to portray the feeling.

2. Once this is completed, both students stand in front of the class. The sculptor holds the piece of art while the other student stands alongside and uses facial and body expressions to convey the feeling shown in the sculpture. Others in the class try to guess the emotion.

3. Have the students switch and let the first student be the sculptor.

Discussion

1. Was it hard to portray emotions in clay?

2. Did you want to tell the sculptor different ways of doing it?

3. Share a time when how something was said carried more meaning than what was said.

Journal   1. What emotion is most difficult for you to express? Explain.

2. If you could have changed anything about the sculpture you made, what would it have been?

Presto-Chango!

Multiple Intelligence: Visual/Spatial   **Grade: 3 and Up**
Life Habit: Sense of Humor   **Time: 10 minutes**
Materials: None

1. Ask students to pair themselves up. Ask students to study their partners carefully for 1 minute. They should notice everything they can about each other.

2. After 1 minute, ask students to turn their backs on each other and change four things about their appearance. They should be given 2 minutes to make the changes.

3. When time is up, the partners should turn around to face each other and see if they can detect what is different about their partner.

Variation   Select one student to leave the room. Give the student a list of things to change. When the student returns, the class should try to detect the changes made.

Discussion   1. Was it easy to find the differences when your partner turned around?

2. Was it easy to think of things to change about yourself?

3. Which was more difficult: finding differences in your partner or finding things to change about yourself?

Journal   1. If you could permanently change two things about yourself, what would they be? Explain each change.

2. What four things would you definitely not change about yourself? Why?

Polite Hang-ups

Multiple Intelligence: Visual/Spatial   **Grade: 2 and Up**
Life Habit: Respect   **Time: 30 to 40 minutes**
Materials: Blackboard, poster board, paper plates, yarn, dowels or clothes hangers, markers or crayons, scissors

1. Brainstorm with the class a list of words that indicate courtesy and respect for others. List these on the board.

2. Arrange the students into groups of 3 or 4. Explain that each group will design and make a mobile to remind others to use the words in the brainstorm list or other words that may occur to them as they work. In addition to the words, they could show a face or a person saying a word. They may concentrate on just one word or use several.

3. Allow a few minutes for planning, and then provide each group with supplies. When the mobiles are finished, display them as reminders to show respect for others.

Discussion

1. Do you think having signs can help us remember to show respect? Why or why not?

2. What are some other ways we can help each other remember this?

Journal

Write a radio commercial about respect. Sell the listener on the importance of having respect and how it can make a difference in the community.

Stop, Look, and Listen

Multiple Intelligence: Visual/Spatial   **Grade: 4 and Up**
Life Habit: Integrity   **Time: 45 minutes (with extended activity)**
Materials: Paper and pencils

1. Divide the class into teams of 4 to 6. Students should divide their papers into four sections and label them "Looks Like," "Does," "Says," and "Feels."

2. After discussing the word "integrity," have teams brainstorm answers to these questions:

   ◆ What does a person with integrity look like?

   ◆ What kinds of things would you see her or him doing?

   ◆ What kinds of things would you hear her or him saying?

   ◆ What kinds of things would she or he feel as a result of being a person of integrity?

3. Students should write their answers in the appropriate section of their papers.

4. Allow time for the teams to share their ideas with the rest of the class.

Extended Activity

Develop a commercial or ad to sell a bottle of "Integrity."

Discussion   1. What are the essential qualities of a person with integrity?

2. How important is this Life Habit to you?

3. Give examples of how integrity is practiced.

Journal   1. What qualities of integrity are strongest in you?

2. Describe a person without integrity.

Look on the Sunny Side

Multiple Intelligence: Visual/Spatial   **Grade: 4 and Up**

Life Habit: Friendship   **Time: 20 to 30 minutes**

Materials: Paper plate with one hole punched near the edge, yarn, crayons or markers

1. Pass out paper plates, one per person, plus a length of yarn long enough to slip over the student's head. Give each person one marker or crayon. Direct the students to slip the yarn through the hole in the paper plate and knot the ends of the yarn together.

2. Ask students to form a big circle, with their right shoulders toward the center of the circle. Students should slip the yarn over the head of the person in front of them so the paper plate is on the person's back.

3. Students then write something positive about each student on the "Sunny Side" plates. The plates can be displayed to remind everyone that we all have our "sunny sides."

Discussion   1. What was the most difficult part of this activity? Why?

2. Why is it important to remember that we all have our "sunny sides"?

3. How did you feel when you read what was written on your own paper plate?

Journal   1. Do you think other people see you the same way you see yourself?

2. Do you think other people see themselves the same way you see them?

Japanese Portrait Game

Multiple Intelligence: Visual/Spatial   **Grade: 1 and Up**

Life Habit: Sense of Humor   **Time: 5 to 10 minutes**

Materials: Sheets of copy paper, crayons

1. Give each player a sheet of paper and crayons. Direct players to hold the sheet of paper over their faces with the hands they do not use to write. As you name each facial feature, students should draw the feature on the paper over their face.

2. When students are finished, have an art exhibit of the portraits.

1. How did you feel as you drew your "portrait"?   **Discussion**

2. Did the portrait look like you?

Imagine you're a world-famous artist who creates self-portraits on   **Journal**
paper plates. Art critics call you a "genius," but you know you're just
playing a children's game. Will you tell the world how you "create,"
or let them think you're a genius? Explain.

The Star

Multiple Intelligence: Visual/Spatial   **Grade: 4 and Up**
Life Habit: Organization   **Time: 30 minutes**
**Materials: For each group, 40 to 50 feet of rope or heavy yarn with
the ends tied together so that the rope makes a circle**

1. Divide the class into 2 groups. Everyone in each group should take hold of one of the rope circles.

2. Tell them they are to form a five-pointed star (with crisscrosses in middle). They cannot let go of the rope or trade places with the person on either side, but they can slide their hands along the rope.

3. This is not timed. When they are finished, they should carefully lower the rope to the ground, step back, and admire their accomplishment.

1. What was the hardest part of this activity? Why?   **Discussion**

2. What was the best part? Why?

3. Was preplanning important, or did trial-and-error work?

1. What part did you play in this exercise? Did you find it difficult? **Journal**
   Why?

2. In what career would this sort of exercise be important?

Eye to Eye

Multiple Intelligence: Visual/Spatial   **Grade: K and Up**
Life Habit: Curiosity   **Time: 10 to 15 minutes**
Materials: None

1. Pair up students and ask them to stand facing each other. Explain that for 3 minutes they are to study their partners and find five things they have in common with their partners and five things that are different. Change partners and repeat.

2. Ask the students to name similarities and differences and record them on a Venn diagram.

Discussion

1. What were some similarities? Some differences?

2. Were there things that were both different and similar?

3. What differences were most important? What similarities were most important?

Journal

1. Do you think most people notice physical characteristics about others? Explain.

2. What other characteristics help us know someone?

Art Quest

Multiple Intelligence: Visual/Spatial   **Grade: 4 and Up**
Life Habit: Curiosity   **Time: 45 minutes**
Materials: Postcards of abstract paintings (one per group), paper, pencils, art materials

1. Divide the class into groups of 3. Give each group a postcard.

2. Tell each group to examine its postcard closely and discuss the following questions:

   ◆ Are the strokes gentle or harsh? Thin or broad?

   ◆ What does this tell you about the painting?

   ◆ What was the artist's color choice?

   ◆ Why do you think he or she chose these colors?

◆ How do the colors make you feel?

◆ Which part of the picture are your eyes drawn to first? This is probably central to the message of the picture.

◆ What is it that makes you look at this part first?

◆ What message do you feel the artist is trying to express?

3. After their group discussion, ask students to choose one of the following tasks:

A. Either imagine a story that might have led to the painting of the picture or create a story that the picture suggests.

B. As a group, make up your own story and develop an abstract painting that would express the story's central idea.

Ask each group to present their stories.

Discussion

Using color, draw an abstract picture that best depicts how you feel today or felt on any significant day in your life.

Journal

What in the World?

Multiple Intelligence: Visual/Spatial　　　　　**Grade: 1 and Up**
Life Habit: Curiosity　　　　　　　　　　**Time: 10 to 20 minutes**
Materials: Manila construction paper, watercolors, paintbrushes, containers of water

1. Arrange the class in groups of 4. Give each group four sheets of paper, one paint color, one brush, and a container of water. Tell the students that they will take turns doing this activity. Provide a method for them to use in deciding who should go first in each group.

2. In each group, the student who is first should fold a sheet of paper in half, and then open the paper. Tell the student to drop a few drops of paint in the center of the sheet on the fold, then fold the paper again and press, smoothing it out.

3. Direct the student to open the paper. As the paint dries, ask the groups to discuss what the paint blot design looks like. Older students can list their ideas on the side of the paper.

4. Repeat this process until each student in the group has had a turn making a design.

Discussion

1. Did everyone think the paint blot design looked like the same thing? Why? Why not?

2. What happened in the group discussion when people had different ideas about what the blot might be?

Journal

1. List some other situations or problems that have no right or wrong answers. Choose one from your list and think of at least five solutions or answers. Would they all work equally well?

2. Why do you think people sometimes find it difficult to accept that more than one correct answer exists?

4 Musical/Rhythmic Intelligence

Those gifted in this intelligence have a strong sense of sound patterns, rhythm, pitch, and beat. Their ability to hear and understand these patterns in music is advanced. Some children can recreate these musical patterns, while others show a strong appreciation for them. These students have strong opinions about music and often hear sounds in the environment—a bird singing or the patter of rain—that others do not notice.

Look for students who react to off-key music and noises in the environment; use rhythm when speaking or moving; play an instrument or sing in a group; remember melodies after hearing them once; like music in the background; and often tap their fingers, feet, or pencils while working.

To nurture Musical/Rhythmic Intelligence, encourage listening to or the creation of limericks, ballads, choral readings, original songs, raps, recordings, sound effects, environmental sounds, song collections, Morse code, instrumental or vocal performances, and so on.

The Teaching Song

Multiple Intelligence: Musical/Rhythmic **Grade: 3 and Up**
Life Habit: Motivation **Time: 20 to 30 minutes**
Materials: Paper and pencils for each group

1. Arrange students in groups of 4. Be sure each group has paper and pencils.

2. Tell students that each group is to think of a song everyone knows (e.g., *Old Mac Donald Had a Farm, Mary Had a Little Lamb*). The group's job is to change the words, using the classroom rules or procedures as the new lyrics.

3. Allow 15 to 20 minutes for this activity. Then ask each group to perform their song.

Option   Students may use a rap rhythm pattern instead of a song, if they wish.

Variation   Use this activity to review and teach content in various subject areas, to review spelling words and vocabulary, and so on.

Discussion
1. What was the most difficult part of this activity? Why? What was most enjoyable?

2. Do you think using music and rhythm is a good way to teach something? Why?

3. Can you think of other examples of how we learn through music?

Journal   Write a song teaching a skill (e.g., riding a bike, playing dominos, etc.) or a craft (e.g., baking a cake, making a friendship bracelet, etc.). Include all the steps for success.

Class Song

Multiple Intelligence: Musical/Rhythmic   **Grade: 4 and Up**
Life Habit: Cooperation
Time: first day, 15 minutes; second day, 20 to 30 minutes; third day, 10 minutes
Materials: Paper and pencils

Session 1
1. Arrange the class into groups of 4. Distribute paper and pencils.

2. Tell the class that each group is to create a class song. The only rules are that the song is positive and does not put anyone down. You may add other rules about length, rhyming, specific content you want included, and so on. Circulate among the groups as they work. Allow 15 minutes for the first "creative" session.

Session 2   At the beginning of Session 2, tell students to finalize their song and practice it. Allow 20 to 30 minutes for this activity.

Session 3   At the third session, ask each group to perform their song. If you wish, the class could vote on the best song and adopt it as the class song for the year.

Discussion
1. What was the best thing about this activity?

2. Were there any problems getting started? What were they? How did your group handle them?

Journal   Make up a "Me" song about you and your life.

Musical Grab Bag

Multiple Intelligence: Musical/Rhythmic   **Grade: 1 and Up**
Life Habit: Active Listening   **Time: 30 minutes**
Materials: For each group—a bag of various noise-making objects such as clothespins, pencils, spoons, sandpaper (2 pieces), plastic lids, small container of dried beans, and so on

1. Arrange students in groups of 4 to 6, based on the number of objects in the bags.

2. Give each group a bag of musical "instruments." It is up to them to decide how to use the instruments to play along with the music they will be hearing. Have them listen to the music first. When the music replays, they should play along with it.

3. Allow time for each student to choose an instrument and decide how to play it.

4. Play a simple, familiar melody. Then play the same melody again, directing students to play along with the music.

5. Repeat this process with different types of music.

Keep the bags and repeat this activity from time to time.

1. How did your group divide the instruments in the bag?   **Discussion**

2. Which melody was easiest to play along with? Why? Which was most difficult? Why?

Music is made up of melody and rhythm. Both are important. Write a paragraph explaining why one is more important than the other or why they are equally important. Give thoughtful reasons for your opinion.   **Journal**

This Is the Way We . . .

Multiple Intelligence: Musical/Rhythmic   **Grade: 2 and Up**
Life Habit: Creativity   **Time: 20 minutes**
Materials: None

1. Arrange the class into pairs. Tell the class that each pair is to find five activities they have in common that they do every day. They should then choose one activity (e.g., brush teeth, eat breakfast, ride the school bus, watch TV, wash dishes, etc.).

2. Once students have chosen their activities, their task is to make up a sentence about the activity. They then develop a rhythm to go with the sentence.

3. Circulate around the room as students work on their sentence. Encourage them to use words with sounds that can be emphasized or lend themselves to a certain kind of rhythm (e.g., We WAAAAATCH TV until we FAAAAALL ASLEEEEEEEP.).

4. When all the pairs are ready, ask them to perform their sentences for the class.

Discussion

1. Did you learn anything new about your partner when you made your list of activities?

2. Were there any problems getting started? What were they? How did you and your partner handle them?

Journal

List all the things you do every day that are unique to you, things not done by your classmates. Which list would be longer: the activities you have in common with others or those particular to you? Give examples and reasons for your answer.

Sounds of Silence

Multiple Intelligence: Musical/Rhythmic　　　　**Grade: 3 and Up**
Life Habit: Alertness　　　　**Time: 15 to 20 minutes**
Materials: Paper and pencils; timer (optional)

1. Be sure each student has paper and a pencil. Explain that this activity is about listening to the sounds around us.

2. For 5 minutes, everyone sits in silence and listens to the sounds around them. As students hear a sound, they should write its name or source down. Older students may wait until the end of the time period to write every sound from memory. Model the activity at your desk.

3. After 5 minutes, ask students to share their lists and put a check mark next to the sounds on each list that were also named by another student.

Discussion

Did some people hear some sounds that others didn't? What could be the reasons for this?

Find a place outside the classroom to sit and listen to the sounds around you. Listen for 10 minutes; then write what you heard. Use the sounds in a story or poem.

Mood Music

Multiple Intelligence: Musical/Rhythmic   **Grade: 3 and Up**
Life Habit: Alertness   **Time: 10 to 15 minutes**
Materials: A sheet of paper numbered 1 to 10, pencils, a tape of excerpts from several different pieces of classical music, blackboard

1. With the students, generate a list of moods and emotions. Write the list on the board. If some of the words are unfamiliar, discuss their meaning (e.g., sad, happy, silly, cheerful, lonely, etc.).

2. Have students listen to several different musical selections. As they listen, they should determine the mood of the music and write the mood after the number of the selection on their numbered sheet of paper.

3. Play the music, stopping briefly between selections to allow students to write down the name of the mood or feeling the music presented.

The discussion for this activity can be a simple sharing of answers for each piece, or a lengthier discussion of reasons for choosing a certain mood.

Discussion

1. Has music ever changed your mood? Describe the situation, including why you were in a certain mood, and explain how a certain piece of music changed how you were feeling.

Journal

2. Why is it important to be able to identify feelings or emotions?

Pendulum Pairs

Multiple Intelligence: Musical/Rhythmic   **Grade: 2 and Up**
Life Habit: Perseverance   **Time: 10 minutes**
Materials: None

1. Arrange students in two lines facing each other. The two persons facing each other should then form a pair. Ask each pair to stand back to back. They should have enough room around them so they can swing their arms forward and back.

2. Make sure the class knows how a pendulum works. Each pair of students forms a pendulum by swinging one arm back and forth. The partners should decide whether they will swing their left or right arms and take turns swinging that arm forward and then back to their sides, then forward again.

3. One partner's arm goes forward on the odd numbers and back on the even (raise on 1, lower on 2); the other partner's arm should move forward on the even numbers and back on the odd (raise on 2, lower on 3). Explain that you will begin counting aloud to 20, keeping a steady beat, and then count silently. The pairs should swing their arms to your beat.

4. Count aloud to 20. Once the counting begins, the pairs should not talk to each other. Then count silently to 50, keeping the same beat. Most pairs soon lose the beat, but will probably pick it up again before you finish counting.

Discussion

1. How did you feel when you could no longer hear the counting?

2. Were you and your partner able to communicate during this time? How did you do it?

Journal

Describe another activity in which a steady rhythm is important for success.

Classroom Conducting

Multiple Intelligence: Musical/Rhythmic   **Grade: 2 and Up**
Life Habit: Alertness   **Time: 10 minutes**
Materials: 3 to 5 minutes of recorded music

1. This is a whole class activity. Tell the class they will be listening to some music. They should listen carefully to the rhythm and tone of the music. Tell them you will then play the music again, and their job is to "conduct" the musicians as they perform. Demonstrate, or ask volunteers to demonstrate, some common conducting gestures.

2. Play the music through once with the students seated.

3. Then ask the students to stand and be ready to conduct. Play the music a second time as they conduct to the music.

Variation

Divide students into groups of 6 to 8. Ask them to form an orchestra with a conductor, string, percussion, brass, and woodwind sections. Then play the music once. The second time, the group pantomimes their respective parts.

1. Is the conductor the most important part of the orchestra? Why or why not? **Discussion**

2. What other groups have a "conductor" and members with particular jobs to do?

1. Describe your feelings as you conducted or performed in the orchestra. **Journal**

2. Do you like to be in charge of things? Why or why not?

Environmental Orchestra

Multiple Intelligence: Musical/Rhythmic   **Grade: 1 and Up**
Life Habit: Accountability   **Time: 15 to 20 minutes**
Materials: None

1. Arrange students into groups of 6 to 8. Ask each group to agree on a place whose sounds they will imitate (e.g., city street, playground, classroom, barnyard, jungle, zoo, etc.). It should be a place where several different sounds might be heard. Once they agree on a place, they should name the sounds that might be heard there.

2. Ask each group to select one person to be their "conductor." The remaining members form an "orchestra." Each member makes one of the sounds they have discussed.

3. Once the conductor has been chosen and each member has a sound, the group should agree on the conducting signals (e.g., hand raised for "louder," finger to lips for "softer," arms waving quickly for "faster," etc.).

4. Each group performs its concert for the rest of the class.

1. How was this activity the same as a musical performance? How was it different? **Discussion**

2. What happens in a real orchestra if a member is not paying attention?

Why is a conductor important to a musical performance? A chamber orchestra or ensemble performs without a conductor. Which Life Habits would they use? **Journal**

Crescendo

Multiple Intelligence: Musical/Rhythmic   **Grade: 4 and Up**
Life Habit: Flexibility/Resilience   **Time: 10 to 15 minutes**
Materials: None

1. Have the students pair up and face each other. One partner begins by making a sound and a motion that the other person can easily repeat. The sound and motion should change volume and speed, build up to a fast crescendo, become slow and soft, and so on. The partner tries to imitate the volume and speed as they change.

2. After the partners have gained some skill at this, have them switch roles. This activity requires students to tune in to each other and respond accurately.

Discussion

1. Which was harder to follow, the sound or the motion?

2. Was it easy to concentrate? Why or why not?

Journal

1. Write about the experience of following someone else's directions with no advance warning of change. How did this make you feel? Were you comfortable or uncomfortable? Explain.

2. Imagine a situation in which it is very important to follow directions without questioning or discussing them. Write about it.

Clap Along

Multiple Intelligence: Musical/Rhythmic   **Grade: K and Up**
Life Habit: Flexibility/Resilience   **Time: 5 to 10 minutes**
Materials: None

1. Ask students to close their eyes and begin to clap in whatever pattern they choose. At first, the noise will seem to be a mess, but if they stick with it, something interesting happens. Eventually, a pattern emerges.

Discussion

1. What did you think when we first started clapping? How did it sound to you?

2. Did you change your clapping pattern? Why?

3. Why do you think we all ended up clapping in a harmonious pattern?

Why do you think that something seems like a big mess when several people are working on it? What can happen to change things so it turns out all right? Have you ever experienced something like this? Describe it. **Journal**

Musical Chair Cooperation

Multiple Intelligence: Musical/Rhythmic   **Grade: K and Up**
Life Habit: Cooperation   **Time: 10 to 15 minutes**
Materials: Chairs, music

1. In this version of musical chairs, the group wins or loses. The object of the activity is to end up with all students seated. It is the group's job to see that everyone has a place to sit, even if it's on someone's lap.

2. Arrange the chairs in a circle. There should be one chair fewer than the number of students.

3. Begin the music as the students walk around the circle. Stop the music unexpectedly.

4. Before you begin the music again, remove another chair.

5. Continue this routine until the students cannot find a way for everyone to have a seat.

1. What was different between this game of musical chairs and the one you usually play? **Discussion**

2. How did the new rules change the feeling of the game? Which do you prefer? Why?

Is it sometimes a good idea to change the rules or the way something is usually done? Explain your answer and give an example. **Journal**

Who's the Star?

Multiple Intelligence: Musical/Rhythmic   **Grade: K and Up**
Life Habit: Active Listening   **Time: 7 to 15 minutes**
Materials: None

1. Ask for a volunteer to leave the room. The remaining students should select one person to be the "star." Students then scatter, to fill up as much space as possible.

2. When the volunteer student returns to the room, he or she must try to guess who the "star" is. The clue is how loudly the students clap. In moving around the room, when the volunteer gets close to the "star," the students clap loudly, and when the volunteer moves away from the star, the clapping grows softer and softer.

3. When the volunteer discovers the "star," he or she joins the group. The "star" leaves the room for the second round, and another "star" is chosen.

Discussion   What was more difficult? Looking for the star or clapping? Explain.

Journal   Make up rules for another game in which one person must figure out something that a whole group of people know about. Name your game and write the rules clearly.

Take Me to Your Leader

Multiple Intelligence: Musical/Rhythmic   **Grade: 3 and Up**
Life Habit: Initiative   **Time: 5 to 10 minutes**
Materials: None

1. Find a simple song that everyone in the group knows, such as "Mary Had a Little Lamb" or "Three Blind Mice." The students stand in an unbroken circle, facing each other, with arms touching, and sing this song as beautifully as they can, without a leader. They must remain in the circle.

2. Give the students 30 seconds to discuss how they will do this. When you call "Go!" they should begin. Repeat as many times as you wish.

Discussion   1. What Life Habits did you use to complete this activity without a leader?

2. Would it have been easier if one person had been chosen to lead the song?

3. What task have you done recently that was easier because one person took the initiative to lead?

Journal   1. What is something you would like to change? How could you initiate that change?

2. Name a person you know or a historical figure famous for initiating a change. Give reasons for your choice.

Place Percussion

Multiple Intelligence: Musical/Rhythmic　　　**Grade: K and Up**
Life Habit: Patience　　　**Time: 10 to 15 minutes**
Materials: Overhead projector, blackboard, or flip chart

1. Explain that the object of this exercise is for everyone in the group to clap out in rhythm the displayed words. This must be done all together, with no extra sounds at the wrong places. If anyone misses a beat, the group must start over.

2. Success is achieved when the group gets through all four sets of words in total unison.

1. Mississippi, Minnesota, South Dakota, Tennessee

2. Alabama, West Virginia, Massachusetts, Washington

3. Alaska, Hawaii, New Jersey, New York

4. Ohio, Missouri, Kentucky, Vermont

**Place
Word Sets**
*(Or use any
vocabulary
words you
are currently
studying)*

1. What was most helpful in completing this task?

2. What was the biggest challenge?

3. How did you handle it when someone made a mistake?

Discussion

1. Please explain the saying, "Patience is a virtue."

2. How was patience important to this task?

Journal

Strike Up the Band!

Multiple Intelligence: Musical/Rhythmic　　　**Grade: 1 and Up**
Life Habit: Alertness　　　**Time: 10 to 15 minutes**
Materials: None

1. Divide the class into two groups. One group is the orchestra, and the other group are dancers.

2. After a brief planning session, the orchestra begins to "play," and the dancers must dance to the rhythm and beat of the "music." After a minute or so, call "Stop" and ask the orchestra to change their tune. The dancers must then follow the new music.

3. Then the groups change places. The dancers now become the orchestra and vice versa. Repeat the same procedure as before.

Discussion   1. Was it more difficult to be part of the orchestra or to be a dancer?

2. How did the orchestra decide what "music" to play?

3. What happened when you had to change your music to a different tune and beat?

Journal   When might it be important to change what you're doing in the middle of things?

One . . . Two . . . Clap!

Multiple Intelligence: Musical/Rhythmic   **Grade: 1 and Up**
Life Habit: Alertness   **Time: 15 to 30 minutes**
Materials: Words to a familiar song

1. Explain that the group is to "perform" a song in an unusual way. Ask for a volunteer to be the group "metronome." This person marches in place in a steady rhythm to provide the beat for the group.

2. Use a short song familiar to the entire group. This could be a seasonal song or a song studied in music class. You might provide a copy of the words.

3. Arrange students in a circle with the "metronome" in the center.

4. Explain that every third beat is clapped instead of sung. Do a practice round.

5. Success is achieved when the group can get through the entire song.

Discussion: 1. How did you feel when the group succeeded?

2. Which Life Habit was important? Why?

Journal   1. Describe a situation in which it would be important for everyone to follow the group.

2. Describe a situation in which it would be important for everyone not to follow the group.

5 Bodily/Kinesthetic Intelligence

Children gifted in bodily/kinesthetic intelligence have a strong awareness of physical action and can perform more complex bodily movements than others. They process knowledge through bodily sensations and are often labeled hyperactive if they are not given appropriate outlets. They have strong motor and athletic skills, are often talented dancers, actors, or mimes, or are adept at manipulating objects and tools.

Look for students who excel in sports; enjoy running, jumping and dancing; fidget when seated for long periods; want to touch new objects; take things apart and put them back together; like hands-on art, such as clay or woodworking; and mimic others' gestures and mannerisms.

To nurture Bodily/Kinesthetic Intelligence, encourage creating collages, cooking, computer programming, displays, jigsaw puzzles, sculptures, origami, scavenger hunts, weaving, stitchery, rubbings, dances, carvings, folk dances, docudrama, models, and stage settings.

Wrap-a-Long

Multiple Intelligence: Bodily/Kinesthetic	**Grade: 2 and Up**
Life Habit: Flexibility/Resilience	**Time: 10 minutes** after start of activity

Materials: Roll of inexpensive plastic wrap, cut into 4-foot strips (wind the plastic around an empty paper towel tube to keep it from sticking to itself).

1. Divide the class into groups of 10 to 12. Have each group cluster together in a tight circular clump. Wrap plastic wrap around the clump of students and fasten the ends.

2. The group's task is to move from point A to point B. This might be from one side of room to the other. Groups should predict the time this will take.

3. Time their movement. If they pass their time limit, have them try again from the starting point. The third time, ask group to back away from each other and try again. The band will stretch.

Discussion

1. Was it a surprise when your group did or didn't make it across the room by the time limit the first time?

2. What happened when you stretched the wrap?

3. What do you think was the point of this activity?

Journal

Have you ever failed at something over and over and then tried it a little differently and succeeded? Write a brief narrative telling what happened.

The Trust Circle

Multiple Intelligence: Bodily/Kinesthetic   **Grade: 3 and Up**

Life Habit: Fair Play   **Time: 5 to 10 minutes**

Materials: None

1. In The Trust Circle, balance and trust are crucial. Team members stand in a circle, facing inward, hands linked tightly together. Each person must lean just the right amount.

2. Still holding hands, every other person in the circle slowly leans in toward the center of the circle. The others slowly lean backward. For this to work, everyone must work together and be aware of what the other members are doing.

3. When the group succeeds, ask everyone to slowly and carefully change the direction in which they are leaning and stand upright again.

Discussion

1. How important is trust to the success of this activity?

2. How did it feel when you began to lean? Was leaning forward better than leaning back?

Journal

1. Balance is important in this activity. What other everyday activities require balance?

2. Describe how balance affects one thing you do every day. Then describe what that activity would be like if you didn't have balance.

Group Knot

Multiple Intelligence: Bodily/Kinesthetic	**Grade: 3 and Up**
Life Habit: Patience	**Time: 5 to 10 minutes**
Materials: None	

1. Divide the class into groups of 10 to 12 student each. Players should form a tight circle, standing so that their shoulders touch and their hands are extended into the center of the circle.

2. At the starting signal, each person should reach for two other hands, being careful not to take both hands of the same person or the hands of the person to their left or right.

3. Once everyone has grabbed two hands, the object of the game is to untangle the knot without letting go of hands, so everyone ends up in a circle again.

Variations

1. Once the knot is made, touch one pair of hands and tell them to release their grip.

2. Ask the knot to untangle into a straight line.

Discussion

1. What caused the most problems?

2. What was the most helpful thing your group did to untangle the knot?

Journal

What are other ways people can get "tangled up"? Describe one way and tell how they can "untangle" themselves.

Silhouette

Multiple Intelligence: Bodily/Kinesthetic	**Grades: K and Up**
Life Habit: Cooperation	**Time: 45 minutes**
Materials: None	

1. Put students in groups of 4 or 5. They should think of something that has happened to them or choose a historical event they have recently studied. Allow 5 minutes for this.

2. Once the event has been selected, students pose as if a photo had been taken of the event. They may use props if they are readily available.

3. As groups present their scenes, the class guesses the event being shown.

Discussion 1. What was the hardest part of the assignment?

2. How did you choose your group's event?

3. Did someone in the group act as a director? How important was that role?

4. What would make guessing the event easier?

Journal 1. Did you feel a different event would have been a better choice for your group? What made it a better choice? How might you have convinced others to select it?

2. Name one person in your group who really made the process work. Explain.

The Birthday Line

Multiple Intelligence: Bodily/Kinesthetic **Grade: 3 and Up**
Life Habit: Cooperation **Time: 5 to 10 minutes**
Materials: None

1. Explain to students that they will make a "timeline" of their birthdays—without talking. Designate a birthday line, with January at the beginning and December at the end.

2. Students may use gestures and signs but no spoken words.

3. When the timeline is finished, ask students to say their birthdays, one by one.

Discussion 1. What was difficult about this activity?

2. What was fun about it?

3. Did you find anyone with the same birthday as yours?

4. Were you surprised by which months had the most birthdays?

Journal 1. Think of a situation in which it would be important to communicate without talking. Describe it.

2. Why are birthdays important? Why do we celebrate them?

Taxicab!!!!

Multiple Intelligence: Bodily/Kinesthetic **Grade: 3 and Up**
Life Habit: Communication **Time: 10 minutes**
Materials: None

1. Divide the students into groups of 3. Two students face each other, clasp each other's wrists in front of themselves, and form a seat for the third student. The two drivers then close their eyes and follow their passenger's directions to turn right or left, go forward or back, and so on.

2. After a few minutes, the students change places. The rider becomes part of the "taxicab," and one of the drivers becomes the passenger.

3. Repeat until all three students have been passengers.

1. Was it easier to give directions or follow them? Why?   **Discussion**

2. How did you feel when your eyes were closed?

3. How did you learn to work together?

Imagine that cars could be operated by only two drivers. What would   **Journal**
happen if the drivers disagreed about where they wanted to go?
Write a story about this.

I Like Anyone Who . . .

Multiple Intelligence: Bodily/Kinesthetic   **Grade: K and Up**
Life Habit: Active Listening   **Time: 5 to 15 minutes**
Materials: None

1. Seat students in a circle. Ask for a volunteer to be "It" and stand in the middle.

2. Remove the volunteer's chair from the circle.

3. "It" should think of something that describes some members of the circle and say, "I like anyone who _____" (e.g., "I like anyone who has on brown shoes," "I like anyone who has a summer birthday," "I like anyone who likes chocolate," etc.).

4. Whoever fits the statement must stand up and move at least two seats away. "It" also moves to find a seat. Whoever is left standing is "It" for the next round.

1. Was it difficult to be in the middle of the circle? Why?   **Discussion**

2. Which Life Habit was used in this game? How was it used?

3. Name some other situations in which this Life Habit can be important.

Journal Write a story about someone who wasn't listening to an announcement and missed out on something important as a result.

Walking Warm-ups

Multiple Intelligence: Bodily/Kinesthetic **Grade: 1 and Up**
Life Habit: Active Listening **Time: 10 minutes**
Materials: None

Make sure there is room for students to walk about. Tell them to follow your directions for walking. There is only one rule: do not bump or touch other students.

Possible Directions Walk around as if you:

◆ Are exhausted

◆ Have just heard wonderful news

◆ Are carrying a heavy box

◆ Are carrying a heavy suitcase

◆ Are bitterly cold

◆ Have just learned how to walk

◆ Are very old

◆ Are 10 feet tall

◆ Are walking on ice

◆ Are walking on hot sand

◆ Are splashing in a stream

◆ Are walking to your royal throne

Variation Ask students to behave in certain ways towards others, such as greeting an old friend, acting as though the last time they saw the other person they had been offended, as though they think the other person is dangerous, and so on.

Discussion 1. How did you show your feelings without words?

2. What do voice and expression add to communication?

3. Are voice and expression always necessary to get others to understand what you really feel or mean?

Imagine you have lost your voice. You have no paper or writing tool. **Journal**
Imagine a great danger coming near. How will you warn others?

The Machine

Multiple Intelligence: Bodily/Kinesthetic   **Grade: 1 and Up**
Life Habit: Cooperation   **Time: 5 to 10 minutes,**
                                                   excluding preparation time
Materials: None, other than a cleared area in room

1. Explain that the class is to "build" a machine, one person at a time. For younger students, spend some time talking about simple machines and how they move. Discuss familiar machines.

2. One person should "start" the machine by moving in a repetitive, machinelike way, making a sound to go with the movement. The student must keep moving in that way.

3. The next student should find a movement that is either a cause or effect of the movement of the first student (e.g., the first person may raise an arm overhead, and lower it saying "Boom!" Another student could stand in front of the first student, touching his or her hand. As the first student's arm goes down, the second student could bend over and say "Creak!")

4. One at a time, each with a different "machine" movement and sound, students build the machine. They can attach themselves to any part. With younger students, you may find it helpful to practice some movements together first.

5. Repeat until everyone is part of the machine. Everyone continues to repeat their movement and sound until "Time" is called.

1. What feeling did you have when you joined the machine? After you **Discussion** started, did you have other ideas of what you could have done?

2. What did it feel like to be part of a machine? Was it easy to concentrate on your part?

Imagine a machine manufacturing something abstract—something **Journal** that couldn't be seen or heard. How would the machine look? What would the parts be doing? What sounds would they make? Draw the machine.

YES! YES! YES!

Multiple Intelligence: Bodily/Kinesthetic   **Grade: K and Up**
Life Habit: Motivation   **Time: 2 to 3 minutes**
Materials: None

1. Ask students to stand in a circle and hold hands with those on either side of them.

2. Everyone in the circle bends forward until their hands almost touch the floor.

3. Begin repeating "Yes" (or "Si," "Oui," "Yah," or whatever word gives positive energy to the group) very softly and gradually get louder and louder as those in the circle slowly stand. When the students in the circle are standing fully erect, loudly repeat the word.

Discussion   How did you feel as the circle of students rose and the "Yes" grew louder?

Journal   What are some other ways people can give themselves a positive feeling?

The Plus and the Zero

Multiple Intelligence: Bodily/Kinesthetic   **Grade: K and Up**
Life Habit: Perseverance   **Time: 10 minutes**
Materials: None

1. Ask students to stand or sit in a circle. Direct them to make a plus sign in the air in front of them, using the hand they usually use for writing. Wait until everyone seems comfortable doing this. Stop.

2. Direct the students to draw a zero in the air in front of them with their other hand, the one they do not use to write. Wait until everyone seems comfortable doing this. Stop.

3. Now ask the students to do both at the same time—draw a plus sign with their writing hand and a zero with their other hand. Let them do this for a few minutes, or until signs of frustration emerge. Then stop.

Discussion   1. What made this difficult?

    2. Would it have been easier if you had drawn the zero with your writing hand and the plus sign with your other hand? Why or why not?

1. What good does it do to try to do something that you feel awkward or clumsy doing?

2. Do you think if you tried long enough, you could do this easily? Explain.

All Together Now

Multiple Intelligence: Bodily/Kinesthetic   **Grade: K and Up**

Life Habit: Perseverance   **Time: 10 to 15 minutes**

Materials: A length of rope long enough for all of the students to hold (rope should be securely tied to form a circle)

1. Ask the students to sit on the floor in a circle and take hold of the rope circle.

2. Tell the students that the object of the game is for everyone to pull back on the rope and then raise themselves to a standing position when they hear the signal "All Together Now." If one student falls, the group must start over.

Note: This can be more difficult than it sounds. If the frustration level becomes too high, end the activity.

1. What made this activity difficult? **Discussion**

2. Could just one person make it succeed? Could just one person make it fail? Explain.

3. How did the group finally get it to work? What might be a good strategy to use?

Describe another activity where success depends on everyone making their best effort all at the same time. **Journal**

Bear-Hunter-Cage

Multiple Intelligence: Bodily/Kinesthetic   **Grade: 4 and Up**

Life Habit: Initiative   **Time: 10 to 20 minutes**

Materials: None

1. Break the class into teams of 3 to 6 people and form pairs of teams to challenge each other. If the teams are small, you'll have several playing at the same time.

2. Explain that in this game, which resembles "Scissors-Paper-Rock," one team always wins over another, mostly by chance, except in the case of a tie. To play, the team gathers in a huddle and decides before each round which role the team members play—Bear, Hunter, or Cage. Everyone on the team plays the same role in each round.

3. Then, when you count to three, all the teams act out their roles. Bear wins over Hunter, Hunter wins over Cage, and Cage wins over Bear. The roles can be played as follows:

   ◆ Bear growls.

   ◆ Hunter folds arms over chest and says "I am a mighty hunter!"

   ◆ Cage extends arms and snaps them together as if a cage door is snapping shut, while saying, "Gotcha!"

   ◆ Have the class practice acting out appropriate postures and noises.

4. Before each round of the game, the teams gather in huddles to decide what to be. Keep a score of wins, losses, and ties.

Discussion

1. How were decisions made in your group?

2. As a class, graph the number of times you chose each character (Bear, Hunter, Cage) and if that character won or lost. Decide what was the best choice for the day.

Journal

1. Choose which you would rather be: Bear, Hunter, or Cage. Explain your choice.

2. Do you ever act like others in your group of friends even though it doesn't really feel like you? Why or why not?

Reaching Out

Multiple Intelligence: Bodily/Kinesthetic　　　　**Grade: 2 and Up**
Life Habit: Courtesy　　　　**Time: 15 minutes**
Materials: None

1. The group should be standing. Explain that you will call out a description of a person and each person should reach out for a person of that description—without touching the person. For instance, if you say, "Reach out to someone wearing red," students should look and reach for someone wearing red.

2. Students reach out toward a person matching your description and then freeze in position. Several players may reach out to the same person.

3. When the players are all frozen, they introduce themselves to the person they have reached toward.

If the students already know each other, they may say, "So nice to see you again!"   <u>Option</u>

4. Call out another description. Keep categories simple and the pace brisk so that everyone is on the move.

Reach out to someone wearing a watch, wearing a blue shirt, with brown eyes, and so on.   <u>Examples</u>

1. Was it difficult to introduce yourself to people over and over?   <u>Discussion</u>

2. Was it difficult to "freeze" before you touched someone? Why?

Write a conversation as if you were at a party as guests arrive. In your dialogue, show both the correct and incorrect way to introduce someone.   <u>Journal</u>

What Was That Again?

Multiple Intelligence: Bodily/Kinesthetic   **Grade: 3 and Up**
Life Habit: Communication   **Time: 30 to 40 minutes**
Materials: Silent movie, television set, VCR

1. Watch a short clip of a silent comedy, or show a "talkie" or TV show without sound.

2. Briefly discuss with students how you could tell what was being expressed even though no words were spoken.

3. Divide students into groups of four. Ask each group to quickly think of a story they could tell in a silent movie. They then enact the story without using words.

1. Was it easy or hard to understand each other's stories when you couldn't use words?   <u>Discussion</u>

2. What kind of messages can we send with just our body movements?

3. How do we use our body and voice to communicate more than our words?

Tell about a time when you misunderstood someone's body language.   <u>Journal</u>

Give Me an "A"!

Multiple Intelligence: Bodily/Kinesthetic   **Grade: 3 and Up**
Life Habit: Communication   **Time: 5 to 10 minutes**
Materials: None

1. Arrange students in groups of 6 to 8 members. Tell them they will be given a group word to spell. They will spell it out by standing so they form the letters of the word.

2. Call out a word to Group 1. They have one minute to "bodyspell" the word.

Variation Instead of calling out the word, give the group their word on a card so that the rest of the students cannot see it. The group's challenge is to silently arrange themselves so they spell out the word. Then the larger group guesses the word.

Suggested Words help, care, share, group, peer, grow, friend, love, like, trust. (Be sure the word is not longer than the number of people in the group!)

Discussion 1. Did your group have difficulty deciding how to "spell" your word? How did you decide on a solution?

2. Did the class figure out your word? If not, how did you feel?

Journal Imagine a place where everyone communicated by bodyspelling everything. Describe what it would be like to live there.

Protector Shield

Multiple Intelligence: Bodily/Kinesthetic   **Grade: 3 and Up**
Life Habit: Motivation   **Time: 10 to 15 minutes**
Materials: None

1. Students should be scattered around the room, with space to move about freely.

2. Explain that for the first part of this activity, each person, without saying anything, must imagine that one person in the room frightens him or her. Then everyone moves around the room without talking, trying to keep as far away from the frightening person as possible without letting that person know.

3. After a few minutes, stop the movement and ask students to imagine that another person is their protector. Again, they should not let the person they've chosen as their protector know. The students should begin to move silently again, this time trying to keep their protectors between them and the people they fear.

4. After a few minutes, count down from five and ask everyone to freeze. They should check to see if their protectors are between themselves and the people they fear.

1. Did you realize someone had chosen you? How did you know? **Discussion**

2. Could you tell if you were chosen as a protector or someone feared? How?

3. Was it difficult to keep your protector between you and the person you feared? Why?

1. Name something or someone you fear in some way. Explain why. **Journal**

2. What or who could be your protector shield?

Racing Chain

Multiple Intelligence: Bodily/Kinesthetic   **Grade: 2 and Up**
Life Habit: Motivation   **Time: 10 to 15 minutes**
Materials: Squares or circles of cardboard (at least 6 inches across) for each team (one more piece than the number of students on a team)

1. Divide students into 2 teams. Teammates should line up, one behind the other.

2. Give each team a set of squares or circles. (Be sure there is one more piece of cardboard than the number of players.) Point out the starting and finish lines. Ask each student to stand on a cardboard piece, with the extra piece on the floor in front of the first person in line.

3. The race follows these rules:

   ◆ Each team moves forward one piece, leaving the last piece vacant.

   ◆ The last player in the line passes the vacant piece up the line so it moves, player by player, to the front player, who places it on the floor and steps forward.

   ◆ The cardboard should not be thrown or tossed, but passed along the line to the front.

◆ The teams gradually move forward.

◆ The first team to reach the finish line, following the rules, wins the race.

◆ If a player drops the piece, or if the piece is thrown, the team must move back to the starting line.

Variation   Some groups might try this moving backward. Judge your group's ability to do this before suggesting it.

Discussion   1. What was different about this race?

2. Was it more difficult or easier to win than the usual type of race? Why?

Journal   1. Do you think it's valuable to do something familiar, such as a race, in a very different way? Why or why not?

2. Can you give another example of something familiar that could be done in an unfamiliar way?

Photo Finish

Multiple Intelligence: Bodily/Kinesthetic   **Grade: 4 and Up**
Life Habit: Accountability   **Time: Unlimited**
Materials: None needed, unless rope is desired to mark the starting and/or finish line

1. This works best with groups of 8 to 12 students. Each group should line up at the starting line. They walk together toward the finish line about 30 feet away.

2. Standing with their feet behind the starting line, the students start at the signal "Go!" and then walk toward the finish line. Everyone should cross the finish line at exactly the same time. If not, the team tries again.

3. The students have an unlimited amount of time.

Discussion   1. What made this exercise difficult?

2. What is the natural thing to do when you start at a line and head toward a finish line?

3. Was speed important? If not, what was?

1. How did you personally feel during this activity? Did you want to hurry the others so your team would "win"?   **Journal**

2. What is it about our world that makes us want to get somewhere first?

Mirror Pairs

Multiple Intelligence Bodily/Kinesthetic   **Grade: 3 and Up**
Life Habit: Alertness   **Time: 10 minutes**
Materials: None

1. Ask players to pair up facing each other. One player is A and one is B.

2. When the activity begins, A is the mirror and does exactly what B does. This is done without talking. After 2 minutes, reverse roles. Keep reversing roles and decreasing time until partners change every few seconds.

1. Did you become better and faster at being a mirror as time went on? Why?   **Discussion**

2. Which was more interesting: being A or B? Why?

3. What was the most important thing you could do when you were the mirror? Why?

Do you think that what you see when you look in a mirror is different from what someone else sees? Why? Describe what you see and what you imagine they see.   **Journal**

Sword Game

Multiple Intelligence: Bodily/Kinesthetic   **Grade: 3 and Up**
Life Habit: Alertness   **Time: 5 to 15 minutes**
Materials: None

1. Divide the students into 2 groups. Ask the groups to stand in a line, facing each other. The first person in line is the leader, unless he or she chooses to pass. The leaders have a sword fight. Each stroke of a leader's sword causes everyone on the opposite team to react.

2. The leaders may use five strokes:
   a. Swing the sword as if to chop off the opponent's head. The other team must duck.

     b. Try to chop off the opponent's legs. The team must jump in the air.

     c. Swing sword to the left. The team jumps to the right.

     d. Swing sword to the right. The team jumps to the left.

     e. Move the sword forward. The team jumps back.

3. Leaders take turns swinging their imaginary swords. Leaders may be changed often, so that all those who wish to play this role may have a chance.

Discussion

1. What did you have to pay attention to? Was it difficult? Why or why not?

2. What was the most difficult stroke to react to? The easiest?

Journal

1. When could it be important to react in unison as a group?

2. When could it be important not to do the same thing as the rest of the group?

Infinite Circle

Multiple Intelligence: Bodily/Kinesthetic   **Grade: 6 and Up**
Life Habit: Accountability   **Time: 30 minutes**
Materials: Piece of flat board (4 × 4 works best) that is 4 to 8 inches in length, for each student (coffee cans or anything that adds height also will work.)

1. This activity can be done by the entire class. Form a circle, with the boards in the middle.

2. Direct everyone to select one piece of board each and give them these directions:

     a. Take your board back to the circle. Hold hands with the people on either side of you.

     b. Stand on your board with both feet.

     c. Step one board to the left with both feet.

     d. Step two boards to the left with both feet.

     e. Then step to the left with your left foot and share the next board with the right foot of the person to your left.

3. People who lose their balance should step off. Otherwise, they could pull others down.

<table>
<tr><td>

1. What was the hardest thing about this? Was it hard to move off your "home board"?

2. How did the person to the left or right affect you?

</td><td>

Discussion

</td></tr>
<tr><td>

1. How did it feel to step off with one foot?

2. How could this activity be applied to life?

</td><td>

Journal

</td></tr>
</table>

Birthday Search

Multiple Intelligence: Bodily/Kinesthetic **Grade: 3 and Up**
Life Habit: Alertness **Time: 10 to 15 minutes**
Materials: Lists of birthday sounds (one for each student)

1. Give each person a list of the sounds for each month of the year (see Table 5.1).

2. Ask students to look at the list and find their birthday month. When the lights are turned out in the room, they are to stand up and make the sound for their birthday month.

3. When one student finds another with the same birthday month, they should link arms, and look for others with the same month. When they think their team is all together, they should stand to the side or sit down.

<table>
<tr><td>

1. Did it take you long to find someone with your birthday month? What made it difficult or easy?

2. Were you surprised to find how many or how few people shared your month?

3. Did you find anyone with exactly the same birthday?

</td><td>

Discussion

</td></tr>
<tr><td>

1. What are some other ways a birthday month could be recognized without naming the month? Design a game using your ideas.

2. Imagine a class in which every student had the same birthday. What would happen? How would they celebrate?

</td><td>

Journal

</td></tr>
</table>

TABLE 5.1 Birthday Sounds

January	Happy New Year!
February	Be My Valentine!
March	Howl Like the Wind
April	Hippity Hop!
May	Mother, May I?
June	I Do! I Do!
July	Firecracker Sounds
August	Take Me Out to the Ball Game!
September	School Days!
October	Boo!
November	Gobble, Gobble!
December	Brrr, Brrr

DOTS

Multiple Intelligence: Bodily/Kinesthetic   **Grade: 3 and Up**

Life Habit: Integrity   **Time: 20 to 30 minutes**

Materials: About five sets of round stickers in assorted colors and three stickers totally different from the sticker sets (or you can also draw colored dots on a strip of masking tape and cut the strip into pieces)

1. Ask students to close their eyes while you put a sticker on everyone's forehead. Choose two or three people to receive a sticker that is completely different from any others. Everyone else should receive a colored sticker that matches the colored stickers on at least two other students.

2. Have students open their eyes and silently find the group to which they belong. They can assist others in finding the right group, but without talking. When all have found and joined their groups, wait until it is clear that there are two or three people without a match.

3. Have everyone sit down and debrief.

Discussion   1. How did you feel when you found your group and realized there were some students without a group?

2. Could you have invited them into your group? (There was no rule about this.)

3. How did you feel when you realized you didn't have a group?

1. Are there any everyday situations when we assume a rule has been made and behave accordingly? Is this always a good idea?   Journal

2. When might it be a good idea to break the rules?

Train Station

Multiple Intelligence: Bodily/Kinesthetic   **Grade: 4 and Up**
Life Habit: Sense of Humor   **Time: 20 to 30 minutes**
Materials: None

1. Pair up students and ask them to stand about 20 feet apart.

2. Tell them to imagine their partners have been their best friends since they were both 4 years old. They haven't seen each other in a long time, but one of them has sent the other an email saying, "Meet me at the train station." Now they are at the station, the train has just come in, and they're very excited.

3. Students should begin by giving each other a little wave, making eye contact, then silently move in slow motion toward each other, until each of them realizes it's the wrong person! So they keep going past their partners, pretending they were really waving to someone else all along. They keep moving toward someone else, but the same thing happens again.

4. This continues until they've made contact with most of the people in the group.

1. How did it feel to move from one person to another?   Discussion

2. If everyone had not participated, how would it have changed the game?

3. Is this exercise easier for introverts or extroverts? Why?

1. What is the benefit of doing something silly like this?   Journal

2. Have you ever mistaken someone for someone else or has someone mistaken you for another person? Describe the situation. How did it make you feel?

The Balloon Popper

Multiple Intelligence: Bodily/Kinesthetic   **Grade: 2 and Up**
Life Habit: Sense of Humor   **Time: 5 to 10 minutes**
Materials: Balloons, a length of string for each person (long enough to go around a player's waist with enough extra to drag on the floor), a whistle

1. Divide the class into 2 equal groups. Give each player a piece of string and a balloon.

2. Tell each player to blow up the balloon, tie it with the string, and then tie the string around his or her waist.

3. When you blow the whistle, the players in each group should sit on a balloon belonging to one of the other team's members. The first group to pop all their opponents' balloons wins.

Note: No hands or feet can be used to pop balloons.

Discussion 1. What was the most difficult part of this activity?

2. What made it work well? How did your team discover this?

Journal This is an activity in which it is important to follow directions, especially the rule about no hands or feet being used. Describe another activity or situation in which rules or directions change how things turn out. Explain how rules make a difference.

Punctuate the Point

Multiple Intelligence: Bodily/Kinesthetic   **Grades: 4 and Up**
Life Habit: Sense of Humor   **Time: 45 minutes**
Materials: None

1. Form groups of 4 or 5 students. Each group should think of a nursery rhyme they all know and go through it to decide what punctuation marks are needed.

2. Students should then come up with a movement, gesture, or sound that becomes the visible or audible punctuation of the piece (e.g., a period might be a fist, a hop forward, or a clap). They need to decide on only one indication for each punctuation mark.

3. Once students agree, they should practice reciting the nursery rhyme and using the punctuation.

4. Groups should perform for each other when all are ready.

Discussion 1. Did you learn anything about punctuation as a result of this exercise? Please explain.

2. How did your group agree on the "Punctuation Pointers"? Was everyone involved?

3. On a scale of 1 to 10 (with 10 being the most fun), how much fun did you have as a group watching others perform and performing?

1. What value does a silly game like this have?   **Journal**

2. Give a definition of fun.

3. Describe one incident in your life that was really a lot of fun. What made it fun?

Elbow Shake

Multiple Intelligence: Bodily/Kinesthetic   **Grade: 1 and Up**
Life Habit: Sense of Humor   **Time: 15 minutes**
Materials: None

1. Have students count off by fours and follow these directions:

   a. Ones fold their arms behind their heads with elbows out to the sides.

   b. Twos place their hands on their hips, elbows out.

   c. Threes place their left hands on their left hips and their right hands on their right knees, with their elbows out.

   d. Fours fold their arms out in front, elbows up.

2. Students have 3 minutes to introduce themselves to as many players as possible by saying, "Hi, I'm _____," while touching elbows as a greeting. (Caution them they are not to hit elbows, merely touch!)

3. When time is up, ask students to find others with the same numbers and greet them.

4. Take turns applauding each group.

1. What was the most difficult elbow combination to touch? Why?   **Discussion**

2. We often shake hands as a greeting. What are some other greeting customs?

3. Why do you think shaking hands became the custom in our country?

What would it be like if we really greeted each other by touching elbows?   **Journal**

Four Up

Multiple Intelligence: Bodily/Kinesthetic   **Grade: 2 and Up**
Life Habit: Sense of Humor   **Time: 10 to 15 minutes**
Materials: None

1. Everyone is seated in a circle at the start. This may be done as a whole group or the group can be divided into groups of 10 to 12. Tell the group that the object is to have four people standing at all times.

2. Anyone can stand up whenever he or she wants, but cannot remain standing for more than 5 seconds before sitting down again. Anyone can get right up again if he or she wants.

Discussion 1. What was the most difficult part of this activity?

2. Did it get easier or harder as time passed?

3. How did you know when to stand up?

Journal Do you enjoy being the leader in this sort of activity? Would you rather follow someone else's lead? Or do you enjoy just observing what others do? Explain.

Who's the Leader?

Multiple Intelligence: Bodily/Kinesthetic   **Grade: 4 and Up**
Life Habit: Curiosity   **Time: 20 to 30 minutes**
Materials: None

1. Ask for a volunteer to be "It" and have that person leave the room.

2. Arrange the class in a circle and ask for a volunteer to lead a series of exercises (e.g., clap, move arms, stomp, wink, etc.). These exercises should change every 5 to 10 seconds.

3. Ask the "It" student to come back into the room and observe the group's changing actions. "It" tries to guess who is leading the changes. If "It" does not guess the leader after three guesses, choose a new "It" and begin again.

Discussion 1. What was the hardest part of this activity for the leader? For the group?

2. Do you think it was more difficult to be "It" or the leader? Why?

3. Which Life Habit was helpful?

1. Who do you think are leaders in your classroom? Why?   Journal

2. Can people lead without being obvious? Please explain.

3. How is the Life Habit of Curiosity important for leaders? For followers?

Touch and Spin

Multiple Intelligence: Bodily/Kinesthetic   **Grade: 3 and Up**
Life Habit: Confidence   **Time: 10 minutes**
Materials: None

1. Ask students to find a partner and stand facing each other, open palms touching in front of them. They then close their eyes, take one step back, and drop their hands.

2. Next, each person should slowly spin around twice in place, still "blinded."

3. After spinning, partners should reestablish contact by touching palms.

1. How did you feel when you had to close your eyes and drop your   Discussion
hands?

2. When you spun around and stopped, did you feel confident that you could find your partner? Were you successful? How did that make you feel?

Think of a time when you lost confidence in yourself. Describe the   Journal
circumstances. Did you expect too much from yourself, too fast?
Please explain.

Intrapersonal Intelligence

Children with this intelligence are "self-smart." They have a strong awareness of their own inner feelings, dreams, and ideas and can use this knowledge to plan and direct their lives. They tend to have a strong longing for justice, both for themselves and others. These children have strong personalities but shy away from many group activities. They are self-motivated and comfortable working by themselves. Their strong sense of self is sometimes accompanied by intuitive or even psychic abilities.

Look for students who seem to know and understand themselves; are independent; have strong opinions about controversial topics; enjoy being alone; are self-confident in most situations; and develop an individual attitude, behavior, and even style of dressing.

To nurture Intrapersonal Intelligence, encourage journals, diaries, personal anecdotes, autobiographies, analysis, reflections, guided imagery, predictions, and independent projects.

Round Robin

Multiple Intelligence: Intrapersonal   **Grade: 1 and Up**
Life Habit: Active Listening   **Time: 10 minutes**
Materials: None

1. Sit in a circle with the group. Begin the Round Robin with a sentence starter such as "I like . . . " that you finish with "ice cream."

2. The person to your right then uses the same starter and finishes with his or her own statement. This process continues around the circle.

Note: A student always has the right to pass if he does not wish to finish the starter.

1. Did you learn anything new about your classmates?   <u>Discussion</u>

2. Were you surprised at anything you heard?

3. Did anyone like the same thing you did?

Describe how you chose what you named to finish the sentence.   <u>Journal</u>

Please Tell Me That I . . .

Multiple Intelligence: Intrapersonal   **Grade: 1 and Up**
Life Habit: Courage   **Time: 5 to 10 minutes**
Materials: None

Ask students to think of something nice they would like to hear another person say about them. Beginning with you, go around the room and offer each person a chance to say what they would like to hear.

"Please tell me that I am an awesome singer!"   <u>Example</u>

1. Were you surprised at any of the things we wished people would say   <u>Discussion</u>
   about us?

2. Was it hard to think of something to say?

3. Was it hard to say it aloud? Why?

1. What would life be like if no one ever told you anything nice about   <u>Journal</u>
   yourself?

2. What other thing(s) did you want to hear about yourself but didn't
   mention?

CAN DO!

Multiple Intelligence: Intrapersonal   **Grade: K and Up**
Life Habit: Perseverance and Effort
Materials: "CAN DO" card (see Figure 6.1)
Time: 15 to 20 minutes for initial set up; follow-up sessions required

1. Distribute the cards. Ask students to raise their hands if they think
   they can bring their cards to class every day for 2 months. Explain

FIGURE 6.1. Cards for "CAN DO"

CAN DO

CAN DO

CAN DO

that a "CAN DO" attitude is worth a million dollars because it influences their life decisions.

2. The class has a "CAN DO" campaign for the next 2 months. They are expected to bring their "CAN DO" cards daily to place on their desks.

1. Name people in history or people you know who have or had a "CAN DO" attitude.

2. Name some times when it has been difficult to keep a "CAN DO" attitude.

3. Do you think bringing your card to school every day will affect you and your attitude?

Write about a time when a "CAN DO" attitude helped you reach a goal or solve a problem.

If I Had an Angel

Multiple Intelligence: Intrapersonal   **Grade: 2 and Up**
Life Habit: Responsibility   **Time: Two 15 to 20 minute sessions**
Materials: 3″ × 5″ cards and a box to hold them

1. Tell students they'll be somebody else's "angel" for the next week. Discuss what an angel might do for a friend at school. This does not mean giving presents!

2. Distribute the index cards. Ask students to put their names on the cards and list what an angel could do for them.

3. Each student places his or her card in the box and then draw a card. If a student draws his or her own card, the student should replace it and draw another. During the week, students act as "angels," with each student trying to do what was written on the card he or she drew.

4. At the end of the week, ask the students to tell the class whose angel they were. Encourage positive feedback about the nice things that were done.

1. How did you feel acting as an "angel"?

2. How did you feel when your "angel" did something for you?

3. Did anyone do an "angel" act that wasn't written on the card?

4. Did you guess who your "angel" was before the week was up? How?

1. Describe how you were treated by your "angel."

2. Was it important to you that your "angel" fulfilled his or her responsibility? Why?

Favorites

Multiple Intelligence: Intrapersonal   **Grade: 3 and Up**
Life Habit: Integrity   **Time: 10 to 15 minutes**
Materials: Paper and pencils

1. Write a category and five or six examples on the board (e.g., in the category of food—bread, hamburger, banana, celery, corn, and lettuce could be listed). Then ask the class for another category and examples. Students might be interested in food, special projects, TV shows, and so on.

2. Using the class category and examples, each student lists the examples in order of individual preference.

3. Give the students 5 minutes to look for other students with lists similar to theirs. When the time is up, vote to see which examples were the most popular.

Discussion
1. What causes people to have different tastes?

2. Are these differences always a good thing? Can they sometimes cause problems?

Journal
1. List the steps a person should take before making a choice.

2. If you learned you were the only one voting for a certain candidate in an election, how would you feel? Would you change your vote? Explain.

Roundabout Conversations

Multiple Intelligence: Intrapersonal   **Grade: 1 and Up**
Life Habit: Courtesy   **Time: 15 to 20 minutes**
Materials: Music (tape or CD)

1. Divide the class into 2 equal groups. Ask Group 1 to form a circle and turn to their left. Ask Group 2 to form a ring around Group 1's circle and turn to their right.

2. As you play music, players in both rings walk in the direction they're facing. When the music stops, each student should line up to face someone in the other circle. Students should talk briefly (for about one minute) about a topic you name. Emphasize listening to each other with courtesy.

3. When time is up, play the music again. The students walk in a circle. Stop the music. The students stop, face new partners, and repeat the process.

◆ Something fun you did during the summer

◆ Your favorite fast food restaurant and why

◆ A pet you'd like to have and why

◆ Your favorite TV show and why

Suggested Topics

If students already know each other, topics can be less general and more personal.

Variation

1. What did you like about this activity?

Discussion

2. Did you learn anything new about your classmates?

1. Which topic was easiest to talk about? Why?

Journal

2. Which topic was the most difficult to talk about? Why?

I Think I Can

Multiple Intelligence: Intrapersonal　　　　　**Grade: 3 and Up**
Life Habit: Motivation　　　　　**Time: 10 to 15 minutes**
Materials: One index card per student, writing utensils

1. Arrange students in groups of 4. Give students index cards for noting a goal they would like to reach. It need not be a long-range goal but could be something like scoring better on a weekly quiz or earning a new privilege at home. Each student should be willing to share his or her goal with the group.

2. Students share their goals with their groups. After each goal is shared, group members suggest a way of moving toward the goal. It could be something to do—or stop doing—or a person or thing that could help. The goal-setter writes down the suggestions.

3. Then the student chooses the most helpful suggestion and says, "I think I can＿＿＿＿ if I ＿＿＿＿＿＿＿."

1. Did others have ideas for meeting your goal that you hadn't thought of yourself? Give examples.

Discussion

2. Which suggestion was most helpful to you?

<u>Journal</u>
1. Did it matter to you who gave a suggestion? Please explain.

2. Do you think you can reach your goal? What step will you start with?

Empathy Exercise

Multiple Intelligence: Intrapersonal   **Grade: 4 and Up**
Life Habit: Respect   **Time: 45 to 60 minutes**
Materials: Index or file cards, pens, or pencils

1. Divide the class into groups of 4 or 5. Give each group enough cards for each member. Students should finish the sentence, "A problem I'm working on is_____." They should not sign the cards, which are collected, shuffled, and dealt randomly to the group. Students who receive their own cards should exchange them.

2. Each person reads the card as if it were his or her own and thinks of a solution. The students then state the problems and solutions. Others in the group offer suggestions.

3. The small group repeats this process until they have worked with every problem.

<u>Discussion</u>
1. Did you hear a problem that you are also working on?

2. Were the suggestions helpful?

3. Why do you think this activity is valuable?

<u>Journal</u>
How did you feel when you heard someone else reading your problem? Did it help you or make you feel uncomfortable? Why?

If I Weren't Here

Multiple Intelligence: Intrapersonal   **Grade: 1 and Up**
Life Habit: Respect   **Time: 10 minutes**
Materials: Slips of paper, pencils

Ask students to write where they would like to be if they weren't here. Tell them to walk around the room until they find someone else who wrote the same thing and then discuss reasons for their choices.

Variations

If you could be someone else, who would you be? If you could live elsewhere, where would it be? If you could live in a different time, when would it be?

Discussion

1. Was it difficult to find someone who wrote the same thing as you? Did you both have the same reason? Were you surprised to find someone with the same choice and reason?

2. Did anyone say you'd like to be here at school? Why or why not?

Journal

Is there value in imagining yourself in a different place? As a different person?

Wall of Fame

Multiple Intelligence: Intrapersonal   **Grade: K and Up**
Life Habit: Respect   **Time: Varies with procedure**
Materials: Photograph and certificate for each student
  (see Figure 6.2), "Wall of Fame" banner

Everyone is talented or gifted at something. Educators strive to recognize those talents in students. When publicly acknowledged and celebrated, students gain self-respect as well as respect from others.

1. Below is a list of talents and gifts. You can add others to fit individuals. From the list, the students select the category that best describes themselves.

2. After each student's talent is identified, it can be placed on the certificate with his or her photograph and hung in the classroom or the hall beneath the "Wall of Fame" banner. This could all be done in one day or over a period of time, adding someone to the wall daily. No one should be left out, for all students have gifts worthy of celebration.

List of Talents and Gifts

Listener, Leader, Pet Caretaker, Friend, Skateboarder, Singer, Cook, Seamstress, Communicator, Mathematician, Speller, Motivator, Problem Solver, Visionary, Philanthropist, Group Member, Computer Technician, Mediator, Musician, Risk-taker, Thinker, Initiator, Actor, Creative Writer, Storyteller, Organizer, Dancer, Visual Artist, Magician, Puppeteer, Reader, Questioner, Athlete

FIGURE 6.2. Certificate for Wall of Fame

I Do a Great Job as _____.

(Place Picture Here)

How Do You See This?

Multiple Intelligence: Intrapersonal   **Grade: 2 and Up**
Life Habit: Respect   **(Grade 1 could do this as a discussion)**
    Time: 15 to 20 minutes
**Materials: Pictures large enough for the class to see clearly, pencils
and paper.**

1. Show a picture and ask students to list three notable things in the
   picture and then rank them in order of importance.

2. Have students share their lists. They should put a check mark next to
   each item on the list that is mentioned by another student.

1. Why were some things mentioned more than once?   **Discussion**

2. What influences us to make decisions?

3. Did you have clear reasons for your three choices?

4. Did someone else list something that seemed more important than
   what was on your own list?

How do you feel when someone makes a decision that seems silly?   **Journal**
Do you try to change the person's mind? How can you do that and
still show respect for them?

Go-Around

Multiple Intelligence: Intrapersonal   **Grade: K and Up**
Life Habit: Integrity   **Time: 5 minutes**
Materials: None

Have students stand or sit in a circle. Ask them to answer a question,
one at a time. Go around the circle. (Students always have the option
to pass.)

◆ What word says how you feel right now?   **Examples**

◆ What word describes the person who is your ideal?

◆ What about yourself are you proudest of?

◆ What is the best thing you've ever done?

◆ What is something that makes you happy?

◆ What is a favorite possession of yours?

Discussion
1. Were you surprised that other students gave the same answer that you gave?

2. Which question received the greatest number of different answers?

3. Which answer surprised you? Why?

Journal
1. Was it difficult to answer any question with just one word? Which one? Why was it difficult?

2. Write a poem, paragraph, or story about an answer you gave.

I Used to . . . but Now I . . .

Multiple Intelligence: Intrapersonal   **Grade: K and Up**
Life Habit: Integrity   **Time: 5 to 10 minutes**
Materials: None

1. Ask students to think of some way they've changed and have them answer using the pattern, "I used to . . . , but now I. . . ."

2. Begin with an example about yourself. Use something fairly general, so students do not feel pressured to reveal very personal information. For example, "I used to like chocolate ice cream, but now I like peanut butter swirl."

3. Go around the room, asking students to repeat the pattern with an example about themselves. (Students have the right to pass.)

Discussion
1. Is change good? Why or why not?

2. Have you made a change that you really had to work on?

3. Does change ever hurt? Give an example.

Journal
1. What is the value of thinking about ways in which you've changed?

2. Think of one thing (not a physical trait) you'd like to change about yourself. How might you go about making that change?

Choose Your Card

Multiple Intelligence: Intrapersonal   **Grade: K and Up**
Life Habit: Integrity   **Time: 10 to 15 minutes**
**Materials: Magazine pictures (of activities popular with students,
    e.g., playing ball, drawing, swimming, etc.) glued to large cards or**

tag board (at least three time as many cards as students). Older students can make the cards as a preparation activity.)

1. Arrange students in groups of 5 or 6. Give each group a set of cards to spread out, face down. (Provide each group with enough cards so there are at least three times as many different activity cards as there are students in the group, e.g., at least 15 cards for a group of five students

2. One student chooses two cards and reads the activities. The student then says, "I would rather _____than _____ because_____ (e.g., "I would rather swim than ice skate because I don't know how to ice skate").

3. The cards are turned over, shuffled back into the deck, and spread out again. The next student begins Step 2.

Was it difficult to make a quick choice between two activities? Why? Give an example.   **Discussion**

Imagine a situation in which you must choose between two things you like. Describe how you would make your decision.   **Journal**

Yes, No, Maybe So, Certainly

Multiple Intelligence: Intrapersonal   **Grade: 2 and Up**
Life Habit: Integrity   **Time: 10 to 15 minutes**
Materials: Two chairs

1. Discuss with students the fact that decisions are often about choices that are neither good nor bad. This activity deals with making such a decision. The two chairs at the front of the room—or in the middle of the circle—represent Pro (the reasons for choosing to do something) and Con (the reasons against choosing it).

2. Give an example of a decision you might have to make, such as, "Should I go to the grocery store on my way home today or wait until tomorrow?" Discuss this with yourself aloud, and model moving from the Pro chair to the Con chair.

   Pro: If I do it today, it will be done and if something else comes up tomorrow, I'll be free.

   Con: I'm tired, and it would be nice just to go home and relax.

   Pro: If I go today, I could plan a really nice meal for tomorrow.

   Con: I could just as easily go out to eat tomorrow.

   Pro: If I eat at home, I'd save money for the sweater I want. . .

3. Provide a question for student decision-making practice.

Examples
- ◆ Should I do homework when I come from school or wait until after supper?
- ◆ Should I ask my parents to raise my allowance?
- ◆ Should I try out for the team?

4. Ask for volunteers to use the Pro and Con chair decision-making process for one of these questions.

Discussion   Have you ever tried to make a decision by thinking about all the reasons for and against it? Did this work for you?

Journal   Think of a situation where making a decision one way or the other could cause something else to happen. Write about it.

What Will Happen?

Multiple Intelligence: Intrapersonal   **Grade: 3 and Up**
Life Habit: Integrity   **Time: 45 minutes**
Materials: Index cards

1. Divide the class into groups of 4 or 5. Ask students to write down two problem situations per group on the blank index cards (e.g., You told a friend something that wasn't true because you didn't want to hurt his feelings. Now you feel awful. What will happen if you tell the truth?). Students should pass their cards to the teacher when finished.

2. The teacher reads a situation card to the class. Working as a group, each person should say what he would do. The group then discusses and agrees on the best solution.

3. Groups may act out the situation and solution they chose. Continue reading different situations or save some for later.

Discussion   1. Which situation seemed most realistic? Why?

2. Are there other solutions that were not presented? Why were they not chosen?

Journal   1. Explain the saying, "To thine own self be true." Do you agree this is important? Why or why not?

2. Describe a problem situation you have handled.

Visioning

Multiple Intelligence: Intrapersonal   **Grade: K and Up**
Life Habit: Self-Awareness   **Time: 30 minutes**
Materials: Writing and/or drawing materials

Students need to develop a vision of what they can be. This exercise can be discussed often to reinforce that vision. The vision should always be based on the students' personal qualities.

1. First, have the class brainstorm the personal qualities they would like to have (e.g., being caring, truthful, hard working, etc.). Older students may include career choices and ways of achieving their choices. After establishing the initial list, ask students to give three or four examples of how a quality can be shown. These might be things they have seen others do or have done themselves.

2. Students choose three of the qualities brainstormed by the class and give examples of how they will do them. Younger students can draw self-portraits that show them using their qualities. Older students might design a mini-poster for their room that they could read each morning.

Examples

◆ I can be CARING by asking if I can help, listening to my friends, and so on.

◆ I can be HELPFUL by picking up my things, helping my sister with homework, and so on.

Discussion

1. Of all the qualities we have envisioned, which three do you think are most important? (Tally student choices on the board. Those with the most marks can be classroom goals.)

2. What would our classroom be like if everyone practiced these qualities?

Journal

1. What will be the hardest thing for you to do to carry out your vision? Please explain.

2. How would the world be different if everyone followed a personal vision?

10 Things

Multiple Intelligence: Intrapersonal **Grade: K and Up**
Life Habit: Self-Awareness **Time: 30 minutes**
Materials: Writing and art materials (paper, markers, etc.)

Ask students to think of at least 10 things they would like to do in their lifetimes (e.g., ride in a hot air balloon, parachute out of a plane, visit Disney World, etc.). Younger students can draw pictures. Once they have completed their lists, have students pick the top three. Have each child share one with the class.

Discussion
1. How many know you will get to do at least one of the things you picked? What do you need to do it? How long will it take?

2. Which item on your list is least likely to happen? Why?

Journal
1. Name one thing on your list that would be hard to do. What would you need to accomplish it?

2. List five things you heard others say that you would like to add to your list. Choose one and explain your reasons.

Personal Statement

Multiple Intelligence: Intrapersonal   **Grade: K and Up**
Life Habit: Self-Awareness   **Time: 40 minutes**
Materials: T-shirt pattern, markers

1. Ask students to think of a statement describing something to make their lives happier or improve the quality of life for others. (Some examples are "Litter destroys the environment," "Gossip hurts everyone," "Love makes the world go 'round," etc.).

2. Tell each student to use his or her statement to design a T-shirt. Younger students can draw pictures to represent their messages. The T-shirts can be displayed as a message to others.

Examples   (See Figure 6.3)

Discussion
1. After the T-shirts are hung up, have students read them and choose at least one they feel is important. Why is it important?

2. Which one would make the most difference in the world? Why? How?

Journal
1. What are the three most important T-shirt messages? Explain.

2. Of all the messages on the T-shirts, which is strongest? Which would be the hardest to do? Why?

FIGURE 6.3. Examples of Shirts

Business Card

Multiple Intelligence: Intrapersonal   **Grade: 2 and Up**
Life Habit: Self-Awareness   **Time: 40 minutes**
Materials: Business card template or paper cut into fourths, markers, bulletin board or larger paper

1. Ask the students to list several things they do very well. They will design a business card to market their good qualities. Some students may play the piano, make friends easily, or know how to care for animals. Any quality or ability can be marketed.

2. Once the students are finished, they can share their cards with the class, then display them on a bulletin board or large sheet of paper titled "Classroom Talents."

1. What three qualities would you want to learn from someone else?   **Discussion**

2. What would you be willing to pay to gain one of these qualities for yourself?

3. Choose one. How hard will it be to learn? How long do you think it will take?

4. How will you be different as a result of learning one of these qualities?

Choose a quality you have but didn't use on the business card, and explain how it affects your life. What would you be like if you didn't have it?   **Journal**

FIGURE 6.4. Business Card Examples

Troy
1-800-CLOWNIN'

Marsha
1-800-BEE-COOL

Put Your Name Up in Print

Multiple Intelligence: Intrapersonal   **Grade: 3 and Up**
Life Habit: Respect   **Time: 30 to 45 minutes**
Materials: Construction paper, magazines, scissors, glue, markers

1. Organize the class into groups of 4 or 5 and distribute the materials. Each person should have his or her own construction paper, but students can share the other supplies. Instruct students to write their first names in large letters down the left margin of the construction paper.

2. Ask them to look in the magazines for words or phrases that begin with each letter of their first name and describe the students in some way. They should then glue the words after the letters of their first names that they listed down the left margin of the construction paper.

Example   BART: – B (bold, bouncy)
                         – A (active)
                         – R (ready, radiant)
                         – T (terrific, tall)

3. Ask the students to share their posters. Encourage applause and then display the posters.

Discussion   1. Was it difficult to find words for your poster? Why?

2. Did this activity help you understand other people in the class? How?

3. Did any of the descriptive words surprise you? Which ones?

Journal   What adjective did you like best on your poster? Why?

Space Zone 1

Multiple Intelligence: Intrapersonal   **Grade: K and Up**
Life Habit: Self-Awareness   **Time: 15 to 20 minutes**
Materials: None

1. Explain that each person needs a certain amount of personal space. Arrange the class into pairs facing each other about 10 to 15 feet apart. Ask for two volunteers to slowly walk toward each other. If either feels the other is coming too near, he or she should raise a hand. The other person should stop.

2. Next, ask all the students to repeat this process. If there is time, tell them to try the process with other people to see if there are any differences because of height, gender, age, and so on.

1. How did you feel in this activity?   **Discussion**

2. Do you think that different people have different limits on their personal space?

3. Why is it important to realize what another person's space limit is?

Can an "invasion" of personal space cause problems? Describe a situation.   **Journal**

Space Zone 2

Multiple Intelligence: Intrapersonal   **Grade: K and Up**
Life Habit: Self-Awareness   **Time: 10 minutes**
Materials: Three yards of yarn for each student

1. Distribute yarn to the students. Ask each student to put the yarn on the floor and arrange it in a circle around him or her to show how much personal space is comfortable.

2. Turn off the lights. Ask the students to close their eyes and imagine how they would feel if a good friend came inside their circle of yarn. Allow 2 minutes for this.

Then ask them to imagine how they would feel if a stranger came inside the space. Again, allow 2 minutes. Finally, ask the students to imagine how they would feel if an acquaintance, someone they knew but not well, came inside the yarn space.

1. After 1 or 2 minutes, turn the lights on and ask the students to share how they felt.   **Discussion**

2. What was the difference between your feelings when a friend was in the space and when a stranger was there? Why? How did you feel

when a friend was in your space versus when an acquaintance was there? Why?

3. What did you want to do when the stranger came into the space? Why?

Journal
1. Do you think space is important to people? How important is it to you?

2. How do you feel when someone is too close or too far away when you are talking?

Vote With Your Feet

Multiple Intelligence: Intrapersonal
Life Habit: Confidence

Grade: K and Up
Time: 10 to 20 minutes
(depending on list length)

Materials: List of either-or choices

1. Designate two corners or areas of the room. One is called THIS; the other is called THAT. Explain that you will read a list of choices. The first choice is THIS; the second choice is THAT. When the students hear the items, they should move to the area matching their choices.

2. Read the list, one item at a time. Then say, "CHOOSE!" At that signal, the students move to the appropriate area.

Examples
◆ A dog, a cat

◆ Spaghetti, pizza

◆ Summer, winter

◆ Baseball, basketball

◆ Coke, Dr. Pepper

◆ Popcorn, potato chips

Discussion
1. What did you learn from this? About yourself? About your classmates?

2. Did anything surprise you?

3. Did the way others voted influence you?

Journal
People usually vote in a private booth where no one can see how they vote. Would "voting with your feet" be good or bad for our country's elections? Explain.

7 Interpersonal Intelligence

These children are deeply aware of other people. They are most at home in person-to-person relationships and communications within groups. They often emerge as class and school leaders. At their best, they interact with people in a persuasive, positive way; at their worst, they are manipulative. These students are good peer mediators because they are adept at identifying others' feelings and intentions.

Look for students who have a lot of friends, are involved in extracurricular activities, know how to "read" others, can usually see everyone's viewpoints, are persuasive, win elections, and prefer to work in groups rather than alone.

To nurture Interpersonal Intelligence, encourage involvement in commercials, plays, friendly letters, role-playing, group research, cooperative sculpture, brainstorming, debates, group problem solving, and re-enactments.

Friendly Form

Multiple Intelligence: Interpersonal **Grade: 3 and Up**
Life habit: Active Listening **Time: 20 minutes**
Materials: "Friendly Form" (Figure 7.1)

Each student should fill out a form as he or she walks around the room finding people with whom they share a fact. Other facts can be included on the bottom of the form.

You might have buddies help each other with such things as getting notes or makeup work for days they were absent, calling each other to work on homework, and so on.

Follow-up

121

Discussion 1. Were you surprised by how many people share characteristics or events?

2. What can you learn about people in general from this activity?

Journal Imagine the whole class had the same birthday. How could you celebrate?

FIGURE 7.1. Friendly Form

Find someone who . . .	Name
1. was born in the same month as you	
2. was born on the same day as you	
3. has the same number of brothers as you	
4. has the same number of sisters as you	
5. ate the same type of breakfast you ate	
6. has the same favorite color as you	
7. got up at the same time as you did this morning	
8. has the same favorite TV show as you	
9. likes the same musical group you like	
10. has the same favorite sport as you	

The Puzzler

Multiple Intelligence: Interpersonal
Grade: 5 and Up
Life Habit: Flexibility/Resilience
Time: 15 minutes
Materials: A small jigsaw-type puzzle for each group (each puzzle should be different and could be made from magazine pictures glued to tag board and cut into pieces), envelopes

1. Put each puzzle in an envelope. Then remove one piece and put it in an envelope with a different puzzle. Each puzzle is therefore short a piece but has a piece from another puzzle.

2. Arrange players in groups of 4 or 5. Give each group an envelope. When you give the starting signal, they should begin putting their puzzles together. As they attempt to assemble the puzzle, players realize they can't complete it. Do not offer suggestions. Let them arrive at a solution on their own. Eventually someone notices that other groups have the same problem. After 10 minutes, if no group has completed a puzzle, call "Time" and process what has happened.

Challenge the groups to do the puzzle without talking.

Variation

1. When you realized you had an extra piece, how did your group react?

Discussion

2. About how long did it take to deal with the problem of having a mismatched piece?

3. How did you come up with a solution? How did you feel when you figured it out?

1. When solving a problem, what is most important to remember? Explain.

Journal

2. Are you resilient? Support your answer with at least three reasons.

Building in a Box

Multiple Intelligence: Interpersonal
Grade: 3 and Up
Life Habit: Flexibility/Resilience
Time: 40 to 60 minutes
Materials: Set of Tinker Toys, Legos, or simple wooden blocks for each group with each set concealed in a box

1. Divide the class into groups of 4 to 7 students each. Give each group a box of building materials. They are going to cooperate in building something and have 5 minutes to decide what to build and how to put it together. They may not open the boxes. Ask for questions before the activity begins.

2. At the end of 5 minutes, call "Time" to end the planning session.

3. Groups may now open their boxes and begin to build. They may no longer talk but may signal with gestures and similar communications. Allow the building to continue until each group is finished.

4. Give everyone time to look at the work of other groups.

Discussion
1. Did everyone in your group take part in the planning process? In the building process?

2. Did you follow your original plan?

3. Did you feel frustrated? Why?

4. What does this activity help you to understand about the planning process?

Journal   Describe a time when your plans did not work out and how you resolved it.

Arm Wrestling

Multiple Intelligence: Interpersonal   **Grade: 3 and Up**
Life Habit: Fair Play   **Time: 5 minutes (including directions)**
Materials: Desk or table, candy

1. Divide students into teams of 3. They will be arm wrestling for 2 minutes. Two students are "wrestlers," and the third is the referee but may not speak. The referee keeps time and makes sure the wrestlers keep their non-wrestling hands flat on the table.

2. Tell the students they will receive a piece of candy for each time someone's hand touches the table. The referee will count each touchdown. It is hoped that teams realize if they go back and forth quickly, not trying to prove their strength, they earn more candy!

3. When time is up, go around the room asking how many times each team touched down and distribute a piece of candy for each one.

1 When did you realize how to "win" this game?

2. How did the whole team become aware of it?

How would this way of playing change the world of competitive sports?

Pandora's Box

Multiple Intelligence: Interpersonal   **Grades: 4 and Up**
Life Habit: Fair Play   **Time: 10 minutes**
Materials: Problem Cards (Figure 7.2, pp. 126-127) and a container for them

This activity can occur on an ongoing basis, as needed. A student chooses a card from Pandora's Box and reads it aloud. The class discusses the problem and tries to resolve the conflict. Answers should be realistic and reflect the Life Habits.

Use problems as daily journal entries.

Invent A Game

Multiple Intelligence: Interpersonal   **Grade: 3 and Up**
Life Habit: Creativity   **Time: 20 to 30 minutes**
Materials: A set of a hat, ball of yarn, and 6-foot string for each group

1. Divide the class into groups of 6 to 7 students. Give each group a set of materials. They have 10 minutes to invent a game using the three objects and all the students in the group. Encourage creativity.

2. Call "Time" and ask each group to demonstrate its game, explaining the rules and playing the game for 5 minutes.

1. Ask each group to share how they worked out the rules for their game.

2. After you had time to play, what would you have changed, if anything?

What part of the activity interested you the most? Planning? Making up the rules? Playing? Why?

FIGURE 7.2. Cards for Pandora's Box

P

One piece of cake is left. There are two people who have not had cake.

P

It's time for your favorite TV show. Your brother or sister wants to watch something else. There is only one television set in the house.

P Your mom said you could take one person to the movie with you tonight. You haven't been able to get your best friend alone to ask him or her. You're in a group of people and it's almost time to catch the bus.

P

You're in a store and you have $1.00 less than you need to buy the supplies for your project, which is due tomorrow.

P

You are standing in line at a movie and someone cuts in front of you.

P

You start to dress for school and the outfit you wanted to wear is dirty because your brother or sister wore it and put it back dirty.

P You hear that a rumor is going around that you stole the answer key to the test and that's why you got an A. You heard that the rumor started with a close friend of yours.

P

A classmate takes your pen out of your hand. When you ask for it back she or he says you'll have to take it from her or him.

FIGURE 7.2. Continued

P

You told your best friend a secret and now it seems like everyone knows it.

P

You sit down to study for a test and can't find your notes. The next day you think you see your notebook on a classmate's desk.

P

You are taking a test and you notice your best friend, who sits beside you, is struggling.

P

It's time to turn in your homework and you can't find it. You hear later that a classmate put his or her name on it and handed it in.

P

You are working on a group project. One person in your group is not helping at all and everyone gets the same grade.

P

There are several people in your class who constantly disrupt it. It's hard for you to concentrate when they are "on."

P

You want to go to a party at your friend's house but your mom says you have to clean your room and finish all your homework. You know it is impossible to do both.

P

Your parents are very strict and don't allow you to do a lot of things. Your friends have stopped asking you to join them and make arrangements in front of you as if you weren't there. It hurts your feelings.

Truth Detector

Multiple Intelligence: Interpersonal   **Grades: 3 and Up**
Life Habit: Creativity   **Time: 15 to 20 minutes**
Materials: None

Have students introduce themselves to the class. They should tell some of their likes and dislikes, favorite things to do, and so on. It is important they include one thing in their introduction that is a lie. The rest of the class should listen carefully and try to determine the lie.

Discussion

1. Were some people better at convincing you than others?

2. Why were some people better able to convince you than others?

3. What were the best lies? Why?

4. Why do you think truthfulness is important in life?

5. How does lying affect relationships?

6. What is a "white lie"?

7. Could lying have any effect on our classroom?

Journal

1. "You can never tell one lie." Explain this statement.

2. Do you remember a time when someone lied to you? How did it make you feel? How did you resolve it?

3. Was there ever a time you wanted to lie but didn't? Why did you decide to be truthful?

What Do You Think?

Multiple Intelligence: Interpersonal   **Grade: 3 and Up**
Life Habit: Creativity   **Time: 10 to 15 minutes**
Materials: Paper and a pencil for each group, object

1. Divide students into groups of 4 to 6. Groups brainstorm uses for a certain object. Each group should choose a recorder to write down their ideas. Because this is brainstorming, all ideas should be considered and written down.

2. Select an item. Show it to the whole group. Allow 3 to 5 minutes for each brainstorming session. Ask the recorder, or some other member of the group, to share the group's list.

Pine cone, toothpick, candle, ruler, paper clip, scissors, pencil, nail, screw, hammer, spoon, chair, eraser, penny, sock, button, saucer, seashell, toothbrush

Suggested Items

1. How many different ideas did the separate groups come up with?

Discussion

2. What was the most unusual use?

How many ways can you use a hair brush? Describe the three best uses. Draw one.

Journal

Eat Up!

Multiple Intelligence: Interpersonal   **Grade: 1 and Up**
Life Habit: Cooperation   **Time: 20 to 30 minutes**
Materials: Small bowls; cereal, raisins, or small candies; rolls of masking tape; sticks or rulers long enough to reach from a student's forearm past his or her elbow

1. Arrange the students in pairs or in groups of 4. Give each pair or group a roll of masking tape and one stick or ruler for each person. The stick should be taped to the students' writing arms so they cannot bend their elbows.

2. Set a bowl before each student. The object of the game is to eat all the bowl's contents.

3. There are three rules:
   ◆ Keep the stick taped to your arm so that your arm won't bend.
   ◆ Keep the other arm behind your back.
   ◆ You may not put your face into the bowl to eat.

4. The goal is for students to realize they can eat if they feed each other. If they haven't discovered this in 5 to 10 minutes, ask, "Is there some way to do this together?"

1. What was the most efficient way to eat the cereal?

Discussion

2. How long did it take for you to realize what worked best?

3. Did you feel as if you were giving up or as if you'd found a solution?

Describe a time when something you did alone would have worked better if you had done it with another.

Journal

Speedy Solutions

Multiple Intelligence: Interpersonal **Grade: 5 and Up**
Life Habit: Courage **Time: 30 to 45 minutes**
Materials: None

1. Divide students into groups of 3. They will hear several problems that might happen in real life and be asked to come to a speedy solution.

2. Read one problem. Give students about 15 seconds to think individually. Then call "Time" and give students one minute to discuss and agree on a solution. Don't answer questions about the problem. Part of this exercise involves dealing with ambiguity and doubt.

3. After one minute, call "Time" and ask the groups to report their solutions. When all groups have reported, go on to the second problem.

Problems

1. You and two friends are at a high school football game between two bitter rivals. As the teams come on the field, you notice the man next to you unbutton his coat. You catch a glimpse of a gun. Security is nowhere to be seen. What do you do?

2. At a bus stop, a young mother and a little boy—a toddler still too young to walk steadily—stand next to you. The boy is fidgeting and the mother slaps him. Then he begins to cry. The mother says "Shut up!" and slaps him again. What do you do?

3. You are walking down the school hall, and see two older boys harass a younger boy. They are about to shove him into the boys' restroom. What do you do?

4. The three of you are walking by a preschool playground in the park. You see a large, unleashed dog jump on a little girl. The little girl screams. What do you do?

Discussion

Discussion occurs after each problem when groups report.

Journal

1. How did you feel when you were trying to come up with a speedy solution?

2. Have you ever been in a serious situation where you had to quickly decide what to do? Describe it.

3. Was there a solution presented that you definitely disagreed with? Why?

Laugh-In

Multiple Intelligence: Interpersonal   **Grade: 2 and Up**
Life Habit: Effort   **Time: 10 to 15 minutes**
Materials: None

1. Divide the class into two teams and line students up shoulder to shoulder, with each student facing someone on the other team. The two teams should stand about a yard apart.

2. A student from one team walks past the members of the opposite team.

3. The object of this activity is to make the person smile as he or she walks by. No touching is allowed. If the person "cracks up," he or she must join the opposite team. Those who make it to the end with a straight face, go back into the row with their own team.

1. How did you try to keep from laughing?   **Discussion**

2. What was the best "trick" to make someone laugh?

3. Did your team help you keep from laughing? If so, how? If not, why?

1. When could this kind of self-control come in handy?   **Journal**

2. Write about a situation when you were somewhere very serious (e.g., church, a funeral, etc.) and something struck you as funny. Why was it hard to keep from laughing?

Simple Solutions

Multiple Intelligence: Interpersonal   **Grade: 4 and Up**
Life Habit: Courtesy   **Time: 10 minutes**
Materials: None

Have students pair up and decide who goes first. That person should make a fist. The other partner has 30 seconds to try to open the fist without causing any injuries. After 30 seconds, ask pairs to reverse their roles.

1. Were you successful? If not, why not?   **Discussion**

2. If you were successful, what did you do or say to make your partner unclench a fist?

3. Did anyone simply say, "Please open your fist?"

Journal   How do you convince someone to do what you want? Name all the ways you use. What works best? Why? Give two specific examples.

Introductions

Multiple Intelligence: Interpersonal	Grade: 3 and Up
Life Habit: Courtesy	Time: 10 to 15 minutes
Materials: None	

1. Ask students to pretend this is their birthday party. Their job is to introduce everyone at the party by going up to someone and saying,

   Hi, what's your name?

   Jane.

   Hi, Jane, come on. I'd like you to meet somebody.

   Hi, what's your name?

   Paul.

   Hi, Paul, this is Jane. Jane, this is Paul.

2. Each time an introduction takes place, both people being introduced should look at each other, shake hands, give a big smile, and say, "I'm pleased to meet you."

Discussion   1. What was the most difficult part of this activity? Why?

2. What would happen at a party if no one knew anyone else and no one made the effort to introduce people?

Journal   How did you feel when you were being introduced? Are you more comfortable being introduced or doing the introductions? Why?

All Aboard!!!

Multiple Intelligence: Interpersonal	Grade: 2 and Up
Life Habit: Organization	Time: 15 to 20 minutes
Materials: Paper and pencils	

1. Divide students into groups of 3 to 5. The goal of this activity is to arrive at consensus. Some discussion of what this means may be needed.

2. Explain that the students are about to board an imaginary train taking them to an unexplored, uninhabited region. Specify the method of travel, destination, and period of time. These can correlate with a unit of study. Before they leave, the students must agree on 10 items to take with them. They are allowed to take only these items on their journey.

3. Have the groups read their lists aloud and discuss them.

1. What were the easiest items to agree on?   **Discussion**

2. What criteria did you use to choose your items?

3. What items were difficult to agree on?

4. What did you do about disagreements?

Describe what your group found when you arrived at your   **Journal**
destination.

Name Toss

Multiple Intelligence: Interpersonal   **Grade: 1 and Up**
Life Habit: Active Listening   **Time: 20 minutes**
Materials: 3 to 5 Nerf, tennis, or whiffle balls

1. Ask the class to stand in a circle. Tell the first student to toss one ball to another student in the circle while saying that student's name.

2. The second student tosses the ball to another student while saying that student's name, and so on, until the ball has been tossed to each student in the circle.

3. Then introduce a second ball, still following the same routine, until the group has worked up to all five balls being thrown in succession, following the same pattern.

1. What helped you succeed?   **Discussion**

2. How did you feel when the group managed to toss all five balls successfully?

Why is it important to learn others' names? Describe the problems   **Journal**
that could result from a person having everyone's name wrong.

FIGURE 7.3. BUDDYO Playing Card Pattern

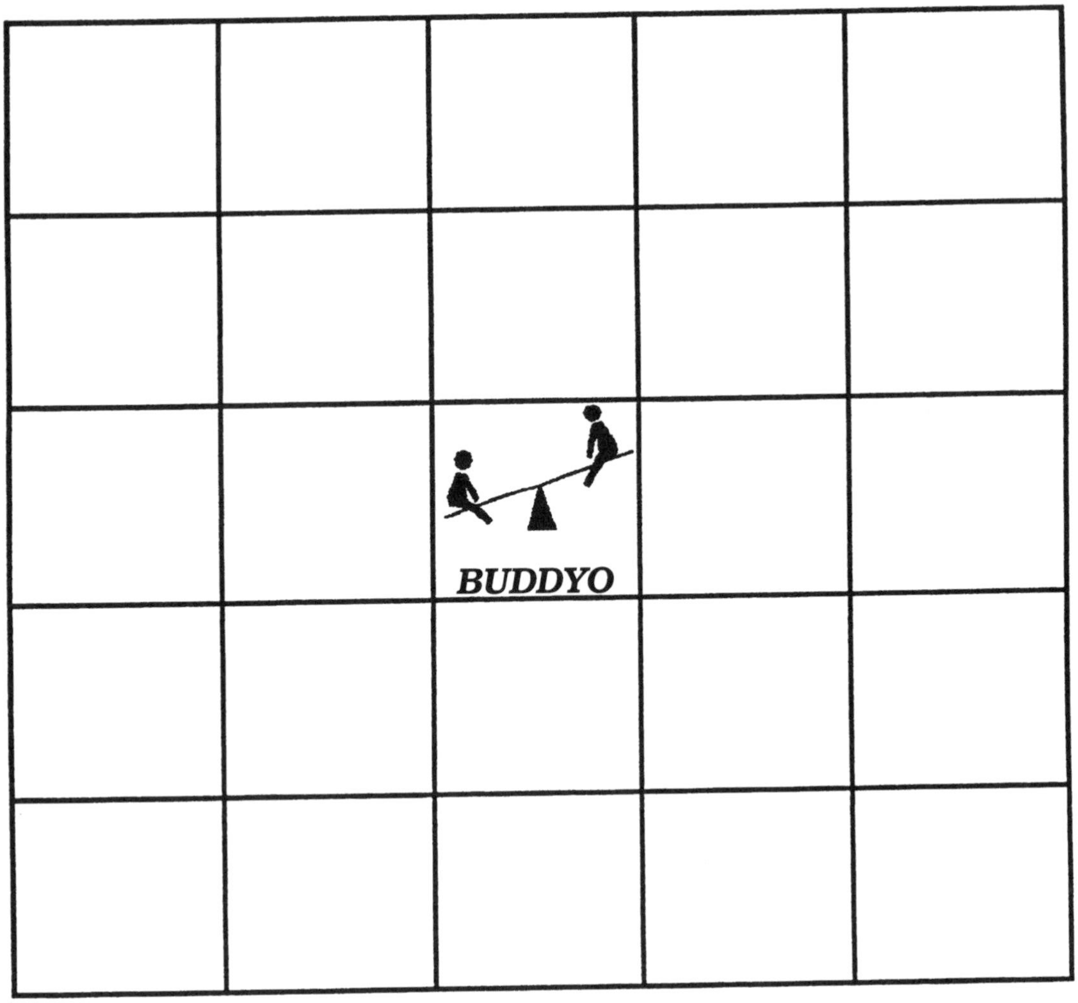

BUDDYO—A Friendly Version of Bingo

Multiple Intelligence: Interpersonal   **Grade: 4 and Up**

Life Habit: Communication   **Time: 40 to 50 minutes**

Materials: One BUDDYO playing card (Figure 7.3) for each student, place markers, name of each student on a small slip of paper, small prizes

1. Give each student a BUDDYO card. Students ask others to sign a square on their card; no student should sign more than one square per card. If fewer than 25 people are present, tell students to draw smiling faces in any blanks left after the signatures are gathered.

2. Give students 3 to 5 minutes to walk around the room and gather signatures.

3. Student names are randomly drawn one at a time. As each name is called, the student must stand up and say something interesting or unusual about himself or herself. Players then cover that name on their grid. Winners are determined according to rules of Bingo.

1. What was the most important part of this activity? Why?   **Discussion**

2. What was the most difficult part? Why?

3. What did you learn about other members of the group?

We often don't know interesting or unusual facts about the people we see every day. What keeps us from knowing more about other people? How can we change this?   **Journal**

Culture Clash

Multiple Intelligence: Interpersonal   **Grade: 4 and Up**
Life Habit: Respect   **Time: 15 to 20 minutes**
**Materials: List of "culture's" behaviors and customs (see Table 7.1)
  for each group**

1. Divide the class into 4 groups. Explain that each group will be acting as though they belong to a certain culture whose behaviors and customs are explained on a sheet of paper. The students have a short time to read and discuss these characteristics. Then, they will act out a scene with the cultures of all four groups coming together.

2. Distribute the culture sheets to the four groups. Give groups 5 minutes to read and discuss their characteristics and ask questions. They should not share their list with other groups.

3. Direct the students to form groups with one member of each group from each culture. Following the directions on their sheet, they greet each other and discuss the topics given on their sheet.

4. Allow 5 minutes for this. Direct the students to again greet and converse with the other cultures—but this time to keep the other groups' characteristics and customs in mind.

1. What was difficult about this activity?   **Discussion**

2. Which "scene" did you like best? The first, when you acted strictly according to your culture's customs, or the second, in which you respected the other person's culture? Why?

Journal   1. Have you ever met and had a conversation with someone from another culture? What was difficult about it? What was easy and pleasant?

2. Do you think it's important for us to interact with people from other cultures? Why or why not?

TABLE 7.1 Cultures for Culture Clash

Culture 1   Your culture likes to greet people with an energetic handshake and/or a hug.

Your culture doesn't talk about family. You walk away from questions about family!

Topic: Your culture loves to talk about food—especially desserts.

Culture 2   Your culture is distant; you do not hug or shake hands when you meet new people.

You like to ask personal questions about people's families; you are especially curious about their sisters or brothers. You insist on asking questions about family!

Topic: Your culture loves to talk about dieting; someone is always on a diet in your family. You don't like to talk about desserts because you can't have any.

Culture 3   Your culture likes to say, "Hey there! How are ya?" when you meet someone new. You're very casual and familiar with strangers.

Members of your culture are very conscious of making good grades and always brag about success in school.

Topic: Your group does not like country music, jazz, or R & B—you like only rock music and talk about your favorite groups and songs constantly.

Culture 4   Your culture is very formal and uses a simple, traditional handshake and the phrase, "Pleased to meet you" with new people.

Your group feels it is impolite to discuss grades and accomplishments in public with strangers. You change the subject every time someone mentions school or grades.

Topic: You like to talk to people about books, movies, puzzles, and board games. You also like live entertainment, such as concerts, plays, and so on.

Peer Pressure

Multiple Intelligence: Interpersonal   **Grade: 2 and Up**
Life Habit: Integrity   **Time: 5 to 10 minutes**
Materials: Dish of jelly beans, mints, or similar small candy; one paper strip per student (half the strips say, "Convince everyone in your group to eat the candy with you"; the others say, "Do not let anyone talk you into eating the candy")

1. Divide students into groups of 4 or 5.

2. Tell them to begin following the directions on their paper strips. Allow groups to interact for about 5 to 7 minutes.

Discussion

1. How did you feel if your directions said to keep from eating the candy?

2. How did the group feel in general? Did anyone feel strong pressure?

3. Did anyone find it difficult to be "convinced"?

4. Did a leader emerge in your group? What did the leader try to persuade you to do?

Journal

1. Explain what connection this activity has to real life.

2. Describe a TV show in which a character was pressured to do something. What decision was made?

Play It Again, Sam!

Multiple Intelligence: Interpersonal   **Grade: 3 and Up**
Life Habit: Caring   **Time: 30 to 40 minutes the first time; shorter follow-up sessions**
Materials: "Positive Statement Starters" sheet (Table 7.2), magazines, scissors, videotape of a TV sitcom

1. Have each student cut out a face from a magazine.

2. Show 10 minutes of a sitcom that uses putdowns. As they watch, students should tear off a piece from the picture each time they hear a putdown.

3. Have students show what's left of their pictures.

4. Establish a "Play It Again, Sam" routine in the classroom. Whenever a student puts another student down or criticizes another person, he

or she has to give two real compliments to the person put down. Post the "Positive Statement Starters" (Table 7.2) to begin the compliments.

Discussion

1. Are the characters on TV different from people in real life? How?

2. When someone puts you down, how do you feel? Were the characters on videotape hurt or upset by what was said to them? Were their reactions different from real life reactions? How?

3. Are putdowns funny when we see them on TV? Why?

4. Is it easy to "forgive and forget" when someone puts you down?

5. Is it ever all right to use putdowns?

Journal

1. Think of a time when you put someone down. Why did you do it? How did the other person react? How did you feel?

2. Think of a time someone put you down. How did it make you feel? Was it a friend? How hard is it to "forgive and forget"?

TABLE 7.2 Positive Statement Starters

I like it when . . .

Thank you for . . .

You're really good at . . .

You make me smile when . . .

I like the way . . .

You seem to understand how . . .

I appreciate your . . .

One of your best qualities is . . .

A quality you have that I'd like to develop is . . .

You remind me of . . .

I'm glad you . . .

I'd like to give you a hug because . . .

I know you'll always . . .

You seem to know when I . . .

You have the ability to . . .

STARS

Multiple Intelligence: Interpersonal
Life Habit: Caring
Materials: "STARS" sheet (Figure 7.4) and pencils or pens

Grade: 4 and Up
Time: 45 Minutes

1. Hand out a "STAR" sheet to all students and have them place their names at the top of the sheets.

2. The "STAR" sheets with each student's name on top should be passed from student to student in a designated path to make sure everyone receives each paper. Each student should write one positive statement on the sheet describing the person whose name is at the top of the page.

3. Stress the importance of saying positive things. Everyone has good qualities. It is a gift to be able to see the good in others. Ask students to raise their hands if they spot something that is not positive.

4. When all of the papers are finished, they can be collected and distributed immediately. Or you may want to collect, read, and distribute them later, or laminate attributes on a bookmark or small card to fit each student's billfold.

Discussion

1. Was it hard to think of positive statements?

2. Do you feel it helped you to know, appreciate, and care about others better?

3. Name a statement you wrote that would make you feel good if it were said to you.

4. Are you going to share the comments made about you with anyone?

5. Do you think you would be able to say these things to another person face-to-face?

6. Why is it important to say positive things about another person?

Journal

1. What was the most important thing said about you? Why?

2. What positive thing about you wasn't mentioned? Explain.

3. What would you like for someone to say about you a year from now?

FIGURE 7.4. STAR Sheet

"I Spy" a Good Deed

Multiple Intelligence: Interpersonal   **Grade: 2 and Up (K-1 if an adult helps students write their "I Spy" statements)**

Life Habit: Caring   **Time: Ongoing for a week**

Materials: Strips of paper, pencils, decorative gift bag or box

1. Explain to the students that for a week their job is to play "I Spy" on their fellow classmates, watching for them to do or say something kind or caring.

2. Vary the time each day when students should write down on a strip of paper what they have seen that has been caring or kind. The students place these strips in the bag or box. It is important to write the name of the student seen or heard doing the kind or caring act.

3. At the end of the week, pass the bag or box from one student to another, asking each student to pull out a strip and read it aloud to the class. After it is read, the strip can be given to the student who did the good deed. Repeat this until all the strips have been read aloud.

4. Students keep the strips written about them to reinforce positive behavior.

1. Did you enjoy spying on people, looking for their good deeds? Why?   **Discussion**

2. How did it feel to hear your name called?

3. Do you think any good deeds went unnoticed? Why?

1. Is it more important to stress a person's good deeds or mistakes? Why?   **Journal**

2. Describe three good deeds you might do tomorrow.

Getting to Know You

Multiple Intelligence: Interpersonal   **Grade: 3 and Up**

Life Habit: Caring   **Time: 10 minutes**

Materials: Paper and pencils

1. Ask students to list four or five things they like to learn about people when they first meet them. Then arrange students in pairs. Tell students to choose one item from each of their lists and ask their partners questions about it. Allow 2 minutes for this.

2. Tell the other students to choose one item from each of their lists and ask their partners questions. Allow 2 minutes for this.

Discussion   1. Did some of your partner's answers surprise you?

2. Did you and your partner have any of the same things on your lists?

Journal   1. Have you ever met someone who spent the whole time you had together talking about himself or herself instead of asking you something about yourself? How did that make you feel? What is a good way to handle this kind of situation?

2. Name something you would like people to know about you.

Skediddle Daddle

Multiple Intelligence: Interpersonal   Grade: 3 and Up
Life Habit: Sense of Humor   Time: 10 minutes
Materials: None

1. Ask students to stand in a circle. Ask for a volunteer "It" to stand in the center.

2. Make sure each student knows the names of the people on either side of him or her.

3. "It" goes to someone, points at him or her, and says either, "LEFT, Skediddle Daddle," or "RIGHT, Skediddle Daddle." The person "It" pointed to must name the person to his or her left or right or else become "It." This activity should go as quickly as possible.

Discussion   1. Is it sometimes difficult to remember people's names? What do you do when you don't remember a name?

2. What is the purpose of this activity?

Journal   1. Why is it important to know and remember people's names?

2. How does it feel when someone remembers your name? When someone forgets it?

3. What are some strategies you could use to remember names?

8 Naturalist Intelligence

Children who are strong Naturalists are keenly aware of their natural environment. They enjoy learning the characteristics of the natural world and can identify and describe the plant and animal species around them. They can see the order and magic in nature and feel most comfortable when they can work outdoors or within sight of nature.

Look for students who enjoy the outdoors; collect bugs, rocks, and/or shells; like to garden; notice seasonal changes; enjoy nature walks; and care for classroom pets.

To nurture Interpersonal Intelligence, encourage nature walks, animal reports, nature collections, classroom pet care, gardening projects, and identification scrapbooks.

Rock Game

Multiple Intelligence: Naturalist　　　　　　**Grade: 3 and Up**
Life Habit: Curiosity　　　　　　　　　　　**Time: 20 minutes**
Materials: More than enough small rocks for each student to have one

1. Let each student pick a rock. Tell students to bond with their rocks and get to know them as well as possible. They might give the rock a name, a family history, a job, hobbies, a nickname, and so on. Allow 2 to 3 minutes for this. Ask students to quickly introduce their rocks to the other students.

2. Have students put their rocks back in a pile. Mix them up. Wait 2 or 3 minutes.

3. Students then try to identify their rocks.

Discussion   1. Was it difficult to find your rock? Why?

2. What happened when two people claimed the same rock?

Journal   Explain the meaning of "curiosity killed the cat." Do you agree with this saying? How can curiosity be a positive force?

Season Scenes

Multiple Intelligence: Naturalist   **Grade: 2 and up**
Life Habit: Creativity   **Time: 15 to 20 minutes**
Materials: None

1. Divide the class into groups of 4 to 6. Ask them to choose a season of the year: winter, spring, summer, or fall. Their task is to create a tableau—or frozen picture—of the season.

2. Allow time for students to brainstorm about characteristics of the chosen season and decide how to show these. Also, allow time for the groups to practice.

3. Let the groups present their scenes so the class can guess which season is being shown.

Discussion   1. How did your group decide which season to show?

2. Was it difficult to think of things to show in your tableau? Why?

Journal   1. What is your favorite season? Why?

2. Create a fifth season. Describe it, telling what time it covers, what the weather is like, what holidays happen then, and so on.

Weather Forecast

Multiple Intelligence: Naturalist   **Grade: 3 and Up**
Life Habit: Creativity   **Time: 20 to 30 minutes**
Materials: Paper and pencils, blackboard or overhead projector

1. Be sure students understand what a riddle is. Divide the class into groups of 4. Each group creates a riddle about a word related to weather.

2. Brainstorm a list of weather words and display them on the board or overhead projector.

3. Ask each group to choose a word and brainstorm its characteristics. Using their list, they should create a riddle of at least three statement clues, ending with "what am I?"

4. Allow 10 minutes for students to write their riddles. Ask groups to present their riddles to the class.

1. What was the most difficult part of this activity? Choosing the weather word? Making the list? Creating the riddle? Why?   **Discussion**

2. Of the list on the board, which word is the most difficult to create a riddle for? Why?

3. Which is the easiest? Why?

Create a riddle or descriptive poem for one weather word not used by the class.   **Journal**

Bring the Outdoors In

Multiple Intelligence: Naturalist   **Grade: 2 and Up**
Life Habit: Organization   **Time: 15 to 20 minutes**
Materials: Blackboard

1. Have the class brainstorm ways the outdoor environment could be brought into the classroom. Write their ideas on the board.

2. Divide the class into groups of 5 or 6. The groups should discuss the brainstorm list, choose the items that could be done, and then develop a plan for accomplishing one item.

3. Allow time for the groups to share their plans.

1. What criteria did you use to decide on "doable" items?   **Discussion**

2. How did your group choose the item for a plan?

3. Which plans could we actually do in our classroom? Do we need to change anything?

Is organization always important to carry out a plan? Give examples.   **Journal**

Recipe for a Perfect Environment

Multiple Intelligence: Naturalist   **Grade: 4 and Up**
Life Habit: Organization   **Time: 20 to 30 minutes**
Materials: Paper (both notebook and large poster size), pencils, art materials for each group

1. Review the parts of a good recipe, such as the description of the dish, how many it serves, all ingredients, required utensils, cooking directions, and so on. If you wish, use an actual recipe on the board or overhead projector.

2. Divide the class into groups of 4 or 5. Each group is to develop a recipe for a perfect environment. First, they should describe that environment.

3. Using their descriptions, the students should design a "recipe" for their perfect environment. Give out the art materials so groups can put their recipes on large paper for display.

Discussion

1. Did this activity help you think about our environment in a different way? How?

2. What was the most difficult part of making the recipe? The description? Ingredients? Utensils? Cooking directions? Why?

Journal

Create a recipe for a perfect class. Be sure to include all parts of a good recipe.

Flying High

Multiple Intelligence: Naturalist   **Grade: K and Up**
Life Habit: Creativity   **Time: 10 to 15 minutes**
Materials: None

1. Ask students to close their eyes and imagine they are birds flying high above the earth. Ask them to notice what they see and hear as they soar over the land. Allow 3 minutes for this activity.

2. Arrange students into pairs to share what they saw and heard as they "flew" around.

Variation

Direct the students to "fly" over a particular city, country, or other area.

1. Were you surprised at something your partner saw or heard? What was it?

   Discussion

2. Did you and your partner see or hear the same thing? What was it?

1. Would you like to be able to fly like a bird? Give reasons.

   Journal

2. If you could fly, what bird would you be? Where would you fly? What would you see and hear?

Nature at the Gallery

Multiple Intelligence: Naturalist **Grade: 2 and Up**
Life Habit: Organization
Time: 30 to 40 minutes, not including travel time to the gallery
Materials: Paper and pencils (This activity involves a trip to an art gallery—if this is not feasible, art slides or prints of scenes from nature are needed.)

1. Before this activity, visit the gallery yourself and select two or three paintings or sculptures that convey something about the natural world.

2. Tell students they will be looking at art about nature. At the gallery, seat students in front of the work (Or, in the classroom, position the art example so everyone can see it.)

3. Ask the students to study the painting or sculpture and find four things in it from the natural world. They should list these on their paper, then choose one item from the list and answer this question:

   > How do you think the artist felt about the detail you chose? Did he or she show it in a positive way? Did the artist do this with color? Shape? Size? Action?

4. Repeat this process with one or two more works.

1. Artists often use nature in their works. Why do you think this is so?

   Discussion

2. If you painted or sculpted this piece, would you do it the same way? Why or why not? How would you change it? Why?

Divide students into small groups and ask them to brainstorm another way to paint or sculpt the piece. Give the group time to sketch their idea and share it with the rest of the class.

Discussion Variation

Make up a story about one of the objects on your list.

Journal

The Four Elements

Multiple Intelligence: Naturalist   **Grade: 4 and Up**
Life Habit: Responsibility   **Time: 15 to 20 minutes**
Materials: Four sheets of chart paper with the headings: Air, Fire, Earth, Water; markers

1. Explain that in ancient times people believed that each person had a deep connection with one of the elements—Air, Fire, Earth, and Water.

2. Ask the class to brainstorm the characteristics of each element. Write the lists on the appropriate piece of chart paper. After all are done, see if anything should be added to the lists.

3. Ask students to study the brainstorm lists and decide which element is most like them. Students should then sign their names beneath the element they chose.

Variations
1. After choosing their elements, students could join with others who made the same choice and create a story or skit about their elements.

2. Students could create a sound or movement to represent their choices and try to find others who had chosen the same element.

Discussion
1. Did this activity help you see yourself connected to the natural world? How?

2. Were you surprised at some of the people who chose the same element as you?

3. Brainstorm ways the four elements are important to human life.

Journal
1. Create an acrostic poem that shows some of the differences among the four elements.

2. Use the four elements as characters in a conversation.

Myth Nature

Multiple Intelligence: Naturalist   **Grade: 3 and Up**
Life Habit: Perseverance and Effort   **Time: 30 to 45 minutes**
Materials: Paper and pencils

1. Explain to the class that long ago people did not have science to explain the natural world. They knew only what they saw, heard,

and felt. Some events were dangerous and frightening, such as earthquakes, volcanoes, and floods; other events were awesome and miraculous, such as the sun coming up and going down, wind blowing the trees, rain falling from the sky, and so on. The people persevered in their efforts to understand what was happening by making up stories—or myths—to explain the natural world. It might help to read one or two short myths as preparation.

2. Divide the class into groups of four or five to choose a natural event and make up a myth to explain it. Allow 20 minutes for this activity and circulate among the groups to help as needed.

Ask each group to read its myth to the rest of the class.   **Discussion**

1. Was it important for ancient peoples to persevere in their efforts to   **Journal**
   understand the natural world? Explain your answer.

2. Although not true, myths helped ancient peoples. Give an example of something not true but helpful to people. Explain.

Animal Art

Multiple Intelligence: Naturalist   **Grade: K and Up**
Life Habit: Responsibility   **Time: 30 to 45 minutes**
Materials: Materials gathered from outdoors, construction paper, glue, crayons or markers

1. The day before the activity, tell students that each of them will be creating a collage from five or six small items they find outdoors. Examples include sticks, small rocks, fallen leaves, fallen nuts, and so on. It is the students' responsibility to gather the items and bring them to school the next day.

2. Ask students to arrange their natural objects on a sheet of construction paper to create a picture of an animal. When they are satisfied with their pictures, they should glue the pieces on the paper securely. They may add to the design by extending lines or forms.

3. The last step is to name their animal picture and "introduce" it to the rest of the class.

How did you choose the animal for your picture? Did you already   **Discussion**
have an idea? Or did you wait to look at the objects you gathered?

Journal
1. What was your favorite animal picture? Why?

2. Write a conversation between your animal and an animal in another picture.

Creature Match

Multiple Intelligence: Naturalist
Life Habit: Creativity
Materials: Paper and pencils

Grade: K and Up
Time: 10 minutes

Students need an understanding of the Multiple Intelligences to do this activity.

1. Divide students into groups of 4. Give students a list of the Multiple Intelligences.

2. Have groups brainstorm living creatures that could fit in each category. For example: ants could be Mathematical/Logical; birds could be Musical/Rhythmic, and so on.

3. Ask students to decide which Multiple Intelligence creatures they relate to the most.

Discussion
1. After students have shared their creatures with the larger group, have a few tell why they picked a particular Multiple Intelligence group of creatures.

2. Did anyone have a hard time relating to a Multiple Intelligence group?

3. Which intelligence was the hardest to find creatures to go with it?

Journal
1. Name a creature that didn't seem to fit into any of the categories. Describe that creature and come up with a new "intelligence" for it.

2. Name one creature from the Multiple Intelligence group you chose. Explain how it fits into that intelligence.

Tree Scavenger Hunt

Multiple Intelligence: Naturalist
Life Habit: Accountability

Grade: 5 and Up
Time: 30 minutes for scavenger hunt plus time for students to use the Internet

Materials: Paper and pencils, Internet access

1. Teach students to properly identify trees.

   ◆ Bark: What color is it? Is it smooth, coarse, or chunky? Is it peeling off? Are there any distinctive patterns in the bark?

   ◆ Leaves: What color are they? What shape are they? Are there multiple leaflets or single broad leaf shapes? Are the edges smooth or toothed? Are there multiple leaves on the stem? How many? Are they situated across from one another or do they alternate from one side of the stem to another? How many leaves are there to a stem?

   ◆ Buds: What color are they? What markings do they have? Are they fuzzy? Are they pointy or blunt? What about them is most distinctive?

   ◆ Shape: What is the overall shape of the tree? Are branches close to the ground? Are there any patterns to the branching structure?

2. Divide students into groups of 3 or 4 for a scavenger hunt on the school grounds. They are to make close observations of as many trees as possible in 30 minutes. Groups should split up and go to different parts of the school premises.

3. Make sure students have pencils and paper to describe and/or sketch their observations of the bark, leaves, buds, general shape, and other points of interest of the tree. Students should also note the trees' locations so they can return if necessary.

4. After information is gathered, give students time to compare their findings. Then they should go to tree identification Web sites on the Internet. There are several sites available with keys to tree identification. If the Internet is not available, have students check with the local Department of Conservation.

Discussion

1. Did any of you find trees that were alike? What qualities did they have in common?

2. Can anyone name a tree you found? How can you verify the name?

3. How do trees make you feel? What qualities give you that feeling?

4. Does anyone know any poems or stories in which a tree has a central role?

Journal

1. Close your eyes and picture yourself with your favorite tree. Once you have it firmly in mind, sketch the scene.

2. Write a poem about a tree. Describe it in detail.

Litter Patrol

Multiple Intelligence: Naturalist
Life Habit: Responsibility
Materials: Trash bags

Grade: 2 and Up
Time: 30 minutes

1. Arrange teams of 3 or 4 students. Hand out trash bags. Each team should be assigned to a specific school ground area to pick up any trash they see. This can be done weekly.

2. Students should make a mental note of the kind of trash they are collecting.

Variation Classes can share the responsibility of "Litter Patrol" within the school. One class can take on the responsibility of picking up trash in the building. If they find a mess too big for them, it is their responsibility to report it.

Discussion 1. Why is litter bad for our environment?

2. Why do people litter?

3. What can you do to help people become more aware of their responsibilities?

4. What kind of trash was most often found by your "Litter Patrol"? What does it tell you about the people who littered?

Journal Think of a time when you littered. What were the circumstances? What other options did you have? Would you still do the same thing?

Animal Search

Multiple Intelligence: Naturalist
Life Habit: Alertness
Materials: Animal Name cards (make enough cards for the number of students—there should be four cards for each animal)

Grade: 3 and Up
Time: 10 to 15 minutes

1. Tell students they will be given an Animal Name card. Their job is to find other students with the same animal. They may only use sounds and movements for clues. No talking!

2. Give each person an Animal Name card. Give students one minute to look at their cards and plan how to give clues to other students as to which animal they are looking for.

3. Tell students to walk around, giving clues. When one student finds another with the same animal, they should link arms and continue looking for others with the same animal.

4. When the students think their team is all together, they should stand to the side or sit down.

1. Did it take long to find someone with your animal? What made it difficult or easy?   **Discussion**

2. What animal was the most difficult to give clues for? Why?

Describe a situation in which it would be important to recognize the sounds and movements of an animal.   **Journal**

Danger!!

Multiple Intelligence: Naturalist   **Grade: 4 and Up**
Life Habit: Curiosity   **Time: 15 to 20 minutes**
Materials: Pens or pencils and paper

1. Tell students to close their eyes and imagine they're camping on the plains in the early 19th century. In the middle of the night they hear the terrifying noise of a buffalo herd moving toward their encampment. They're in grave danger!

2. BUT they can bring any individual from history into their situation to help them out.

3. Ask students to write down the name of the person they would choose and list at least one reason for their choice. Allow about 5 minutes for this.

4. Then ask students to go around the room and see if they can find other students who chose the same person as they did and compare reasons for their choice.

Ask students to choose a person from a specific unit of history or literature.   **Variation**

1. How many chose the same person as you? Why were there so many or so few?   **Discussion**

2. What were the best reasons people gave for their choices?

If you could have dinner with any person from any period of time, whom would you choose? Why?   **Journal**

Nature Quest

Multiple Intelligence: Naturalist
Life Habit: Curiosity
Materials: Paper and pencils

Grade: K and Up
Time: 10 minutes
for brainstorming

1. Put students in small groups to brainstorm questions they have about nature (e.g., What is lightning? Why do trees have rings? How do worms move through the earth?). Make a class list of all the questions, specially noting any repeated by the groups.

2. Allow students to choose the question they most want to research. Depending on interest, you may have students working together in groups. You may bring in materials, visit the library, bring in local experts, or use the Internet or any other available means of discovering answers. There may be one question so popular that you explore it together as a class. This activity can continue for as long as you like, even over several months, with Nature Quest exploration happening each week at a specific time.

3. When students finish their research, set up a Nature Quest bulletin board in the hall so the school may enjoy the benefits of the students' work. Each "quest" should have the illustrated question on a page for everyone to see. The answer should be on the page underneath this cover sheet.

Discussion
1. What resources were most helpful to you?
2. Did you have a question that you never found the answer to?
3. What did you enjoy most about this activity?

Journal List two more questions about nature you would like to explore. Choose one of the questions and write a "far-out" explanation created from your imagination.

Picture This

Multiple Intelligence: Naturalist
Life Habit: Creativity
Materials: Drawing materials

Grade: K and Up
Time: 45 minutes

1. Show students pictures of cave drawings and explain why this communication was used and what it tells us about people and events. Students will create their own "cave drawing" in this activity.

2. Because prehistoric people lived in nature, have students imagine what might have taken place on this very spot millions of years ago. Their stories should begin with an image from the past and have a beginning, a middle, and an end. Once they have a story in mind, the students can begin drawing—frame by frame. Their pictures should give the main idea of the story.

3. When everyone is finished, create a classroom "cave." Hang the drawings on the wall for students to view. Afterward, they can sit in a circle and tell their stories.

1. Was it hard to imagine yourself in prehistoric times?   **Discussion**

2. Could you understand the stories just by looking at them?

Tell one of your family stories by drawing pictures.   **Journal**

Rubbings

Multiple Intelligence: Naturalist   **Grade: K and Up**
Life Habit: Alertness   **Time: 45 minutes**
Materials: Paper and pencils

1. Take students outside to find 10 things in nature with different textures.

2. When possible, the students should make rubbings to capture the texture on paper. If a rubbing is not possible (as with a caterpillar, etc.), they should draw the object.

3. They should then list adjectives next to the rubbing or drawing to describe the texture. Give older students time with a thesaurus to better refine their adjective list.

1. Which texture did you like the most? The least?   **Discussion**

2. What was your favorite adjective?

3. Was there a texture you couldn't capture very well with words? If someone shares one, ask if others can suggest descriptors that give a clearer image.

1. Make a list of good descriptor words you heard today.   **Journal**

2. Describe in detail a distinct memory of something you have touched, smelled, or seen in the past.

Index

CORWIN
PRESS

The Corwin Press logo—a raven striding across an open book—represents the happy union of courage and learning. We are a professional-level publisher of books and journals for K–12 educators, and we are committed to creating and providing resources that embody these qualities. Corwin's motto is "Success for All Learners."